What's the Best Trivia Book?

Over 3,000 Questions in 12 Categories

David Fickes

Introduction

By nature, I tend to collect trivia without trying. Until relatively recently, I had never sought out trivia; however, after creating a holiday trivia presentation for a community party and then showing it at one of our fitness studio spinning classes, I found myself creating weekly trivia. The cycling clients enjoyed the diversion of answering questions while they exercised, so I continued.

What you find in most trivia is a lot of erroneous or outdated information or questions that are so simple or esoteric that they aren't interesting. It is difficult to come up with interesting questions that are at the right level of difficulty that a wide variety of people can enjoy them, and they are something that you feel you should know or want to know.

I have tried to ensure that the information is as accurate as possible, and to retain its accuracy, I have also tried to avoid questions whose answers can quickly change with time. Since the simple answer is often not all you want to know, the answers also frequently include additional details to put them in context and provide further information.

There are over 3,000 questions in 12 wide-ranging categories – Animals, Arts, History, Literature, Miscellaneous, Movies, Science and Nature, Sports, Television, U.S. Geography, U.S. Presidents, and World Geography. To make it quick and easy to test yourself or others without initially seeing the answers, each category is divided into short quizzes with 10 questions followed by their answers; there are 325 total quizzes.

This is book 1 of my *What's the Best Trivia?* series; I hope you enjoy it, and if you do, look for other books in the series covering a variety of trivia topics.

Contents

Animals..1

Arts...19

History 35

Literature..65

Miscellaneous 89

Movies..118

Science and Nature 151

Sports...173

Television 191

U.S. Geography..216

U.S. Presidents 230

World Geography 244

Animals

Quiz 1

1) What is the offspring of a cob and a pen?
2) What is a monotreme?
3) What is a bird's vocal organ called?
4) What is the largest venomous snake?
5) How many toes does a rhinoceros have on each foot?
6) What order of mammals has the most species?
7) The Komodo dragon is native to what country?
8) What was the first animal placed on the endangered species list?
9) What two islands are the natural habitat of the orangutan?
10) How many eyelids do camels have?

Quiz 1 Answers

1) Swan
2) Egg laying mammal
3) Syrinx
4) King cobra
5) Three
6) Rodents
7) Indonesia
8) Peregrine falcon
9) Borneo and Sumatra
10) Three – for sand protection

Quiz 2

1) What color is octopus blood?
2) What is the fastest swimming fish?
3) Only one species of bear is almost exclusively carnivorous, and only one species is almost exclusively herbivorous; what are these two species?

4) What male fish species give birth?

5) Ribbon worms will do what if they can't find food?

6) What bird has the largest wingspan?

7) How many pairs of legs does a shrimp have?

8) What two animals are on the Australian coat of arms?

9) Alligators are naturally found in the United States and what other country?

10) What is the only female animal that has antlers?

Quiz 2 Answers

1) Blue – A copper rich protein carries oxygen instead of the iron rich protein in other animals.

2) Sailfish – 68 mph

3) Polar bear and giant panda

4) Seahorse and pipefish

5) Eat themselves; they can eat a substantial portion of their own body and still survive.

6) Albatross – up to over 11 feet

7) Five

8) Emu and kangaroo

9) China

10) Caribou or reindeer

Quiz 3

1) What fish's name is thought to derive from the Latin meaning "to leap"?

2) What is the largest species of deer?

3) What lives in a formicary?

4) What did ancient Egyptians do to mourn the deaths of their cats?

5) What is a rhinoceros horn made of?

6) What animal has the world's longest distance migration?

7) What animal lives in a drey?

8) Along with some species of sharks, what common ocean fish needs to swim continuously to breathe?

Animals

9) What is the heaviest snake?

10) What is the only snake that builds a nest?

Quiz 3 Answers

1) Salmon
2) Moose – up to 7 feet tall and 1,500 pounds
3) Ants
4) They shaved off their own eyebrows.
5) Hair
6) Sooty shearwater – It is one of the most common seabirds in the world and has been tracked electronically migrating 40,000 miles.
7) Squirrel
8) Tuna – They can't pump water through their gills without swimming.
9) Anaconda – up to 550 pounds
10) King cobra – It lays up to 40 eggs at once and builds a nest from vegetation to help keep the eggs safe.

Quiz 4

1) Fireflies are what kind of insect?
2) What fish is known as poor man's lobster?
3) What breed of dog can't bark?
4) What type of creature lives in a sett?
5) What kind of animal does cashmere come from?
6) What do insects do with their spiracles?
7) Other than elephants, what is the heaviest land animal?
8) What is the only insect that can turn its head?
9) The male of what species testicles explode on mating and then dies?
10) What kind of whale is Moby Dick?

Quiz 4 Answers

1) Beetle
2) Monk fish

3) Basenji
4) Badger
5) Goat
6) Breathe
7) Rhinoceros
8) Praying mantis
9) Honeybee
10) Sperm whale

Quiz 5

1) What animal has the most taste buds?
2) Of all the animal species scientists have studied, what is the only one that shows no outward signs of conciliatory behavior?
3) What breed of dog, known for its thick white coat, is named for the nomadic people of Siberia who bred it?
4) What creature can be Indian, White, or Broad Lipped?
5) What mammal has the shortest known gestation period with an average of just 12 days?
6) What is the largest land predator?
7) What is the more common name of the chaparral cock?
8) Owls have how many eyelids?
9) What species of animal has sub-species including Masai, Reticulated, and Rothschild's?
10) Armadillos are good swimmers, but what other method do they use to cross bodies of water?

Quiz 5 Answers

1) Catfish – It has over 100,000 taste buds both in its mouth and all over its body, about 10 times more than humans.
2) Domestic cat
3) Samoyed
4) Rhinoceros
5) Opossum
6) Polar bear – up to 11 feet long and 1,700 pounds

7) Roadrunner

8) Three – They have one for blinking, one for sleeping, and one for keeping their eyes clean.

9) Giraffe

10) They walk underwater; they can hold their breath for six to eight minutes.

Quiz 6

1) Oysters can change what about themselves based on environmental conditions?

2) What animal's name translates from Arabic as "fast walker"?

3) What is the largest invertebrate (animal without a backbone) species?

4) What animal has the longest known lifespan of all vertebrate (animals with a backbone) species?

5) An elephant is a pachyderm; what does pachyderm literally mean?

6) What is unique about a crocodile's tongue?

7) A female cat is called a molly; after she has become a mother, what is she called?

8) What is the heaviest bird capable of flight?

9) What is unusual about a cat's jaw?

10) Besides elephants and rhinoceroses, what other animals are considered pachyderms?

Quiz 6 Answers

1) Gender – It can change back and forth based on conditions.

2) Giraffe

3) Colossal squid

4) Greenland shark – 400 years

5) Thick skinned

6) They can't stick it out; it is attached to the roof of their mouth; their tongue helps keep their throat closed underwater, so they can open their mouth to hunt prey.

7) A queen

8) Kori bustard – It is from Africa and weighs about 40 pounds.

9) It can't move sideways, so they can't chew large chunks.

10) Hippopotamuses

Quiz 7

1) What is the name for a group of elk?

2) Adult domestic cats meow for what purpose?

3) At what age does a filly become a mare?

4) What is a group of rhinoceros called?

5) Humans have seven neck vertebrae; how many do giraffes have?

6) Birds don't have what basic body function of most animals?

7) Horses can't do what normal body function through their mouths?

8) What is the only animal that naturally has an odd number of whiskers?

9) Why are bald eagles called bald when they aren't?

10) How many legs do butterflies have?

Quiz 7 Answers

1) Gang

2) To communicate with humans - They don't meow to each other.

3) Five

4) Crash

5) Seven

6) They don't urinate. Birds convert excess nitrogen to uric acid instead of urea; it is less toxic and doesn't need to be diluted as much. It goes out with their other waste and saves water, so they don't have to drink as much.

7) Breathe – A soft palate blocks off the pharynx from the mouth except when swallowing.

8) Catfish

9) Bald comes from the old English word piebald which means white headed.

10) Six

Quiz 8

1) Including hunting dives, what is the fastest bird in the world?

2) Where is the only place in the world that alligators and crocodiles exist together naturally in the wild?

3) What is the largest lizard?

4) What is the national animal of Scotland?

5) What country has the largest population of poisonous snakes?

6) What is the most common group of insects?

7) Iguanas have three of something that most animals have two; what is it?

8) Lemurs are native to what island nation?

9) What animal has the longest tongue relative to its size?

10) What is the sleepiest animal in the world?

Quiz 8 Answers

1) Peregrine falcon – 242 mph

2) Southern Florida

3) Komodo dragon – up to 10 feet long and 250 pounds

4) Unicorn

5) Australia

6) Beetles – followed by flies

7) Eyes – A third parietal eye on top of their head can just distinguish light and dark.

8) Madagascar

9) Chameleon

10) Koala – It sleeps 22 hours per day.

Quiz 9

1) What shark is thought to be the largest to have ever lived on Earth?

2) What is the world's largest reptile?

3) What animal can survive temperatures from −458 to 300 degrees Fahrenheit, 1,000 atmospheres of pressure, radiation hundreds of times higher than the lethal dose for humans, the vacuum of space, and can live for 30 years without food or water?

4) What kind of animal lives in a holt?

5) What is the world's largest rodent?

6) What is the fastest moving land snake?

7) What animal has the world's largest egg?

8) What color is a polar bear's skin?

9) What happens to a bear's urine when they hibernate?

10) What is the largest animal ever known to have lived on Earth?

Quiz 9 Answers

1) Megalodon – It became extinct about 2.6 million years ago and was up to 59 feet long and 65 tons.

2) Saltwater crocodile – up to 20 feet long and 3,000 pounds

3) Tardigrade – They are water dwelling, eight-legged micro (about 0.02 inches long) animals that were discovered in 1773 and are found everywhere from mountain tops to the deep sea and from tropical rainforests to the Antarctic.

4) Otter

5) Capybara – up to 150 pounds

6) Black mamba – 12 mph

7) Whale shark – The ostrich has the largest laid egg.

8) Black

9) They don't urinate in hibernation; their body converts the urine into protein, and they use it as food.

10) Blue whale – up to 100 feet long and 200 tons

Quiz 10

1) What is the largest current day shark?

2) What animal has the largest brain?

3) What bird species is the highest flying ever recorded?

4) Why is a giraffe's tongue black or purple?

5) What animal has the most legs?

6) A flamboyance is a group of what animals?

7) What do sea otters do while they are sleeping, so they don't drift apart?

8) In terms of the senses, what do most birds lack?

9) What is the fastest two-legged animal?

10) If cats are feline, what are sheep?

Quiz 10 Answers

1) Whale shark – up to 41 feet long and 47,000 pounds
2) Sperm whale – 17 pounds
3) Ruppell's griffon vulture – It has been spotted at 37,000 feet; they have special hemoglobin that makes their oxygen intake more effective.
4) To prevent sunburn - It is exposed a lot of the time while they eat.
5) Millipede – up to 750
6) Flamingos
7) Hold hands
8) Sense of smell
9) Ostrich – over 40 mph
10) Ovine

Quiz 11

1) The U.S. has the most dogs of any country in the world; what country has the second most?
2) The U.S. has the most domestic cats of any country in the world; what country has the second most?
3) What land animal has the longest tail?
4) What part of their bodies do butterflies taste with?
5) What is the V-shaped formation of a flock of geese called?
6) What is nidification?
7) You can tell the age of a whale by counting the rings in its what?
8) What is unusual about grey whale mating habits?
9) What animal produces the loudest sound?
10) The okapi belongs to what family of animals?

Quiz 11 Answers

1) Brazil
2) China
3) Giraffe – up to eight feet long

4) Feet

5) Skein

6) Nest building

7) Earwax

8) They always mate in a threesome with two males and one female. One of the males is dominant, and the other assists.

9) Sperm whale – 230 decibels

10) Giraffe

Quiz 12

1) Killer whales aren't whales; what are they?

2) What percent of kangaroos are left handed?

3) During WWI, the British army tried to train what animal to battle submarines?

4) When a woodpecker's beak hits a tree, how many times the force of gravity does it experience?

5) What animal has the greatest bite force?

6) What is the only insect considered kosher?

7) How many species of insect are native to Antarctica?

8) How old was the world's oldest dog?

9) How many blood types do dogs have?

10) What are the only two animal species known to seek visual clues from another animal's eyes?

Quiz 12 Answers

1) Dolphins – The similarities with dolphins include teeth, streamlined bodies, rounded head, beak, echolocation, living in pods, and group hunting.

2) Almost 100%

3) Seagulls – They were supposed to poop on periscopes.

4) 1,000 times

5) Nile crocodile – 5,000 psi

6) Locust

7) One – Antarctic midge

8) 29 years

9) 13

10) Humans and dogs

Quiz 13

1) Humans need 16 to 20 images per second to perceive something as a moving picture rather than a flickering image; how may images per second do dogs need?

2) On average, how many people do sharks kill per year?

3) What happens as soon as sand tiger shark embryos develop teeth while still in the womb?

4) Female Greenland sharks reach sexual maturity at what age?

5) Why don't sharks get cavities?

6) What country has the world's largest feral camel herd?

7) What country has all 10 of the deadliest snakes in the world?

8) How many species of bear are alive today?

9) What is a group of bears called?

10) Scientists believe that herrings use what unusual method to communicate?

Quiz 13 Answers

1) 70 – Older televisions could only produce 50 images per second, so dogs would only see flickering images; modern televisions are fast enough to appear as moving pictures to dogs.

2) 12

3) The largest of the embryos in each of the two uteruses attacks and eats its siblings leaving just two pups to be born.

4) 150 – Greenland sharks grow to similar size as great whites and can live up to 400 years.

5) The outside of their teeth is made of fluoride.

6) Australia – There were as many as 1 million camels at one time; they were imported in the 19th century and many were later set free as the automobile took over. They roam freely with no natural predators.

7) Australia

8) Eight – sun, sloth, spectacled, American black, Asian black, brown,

polar, giant panda

9) A sloth

10) Farts – Herrings have excellent hearing and their farts produce a high-pitched sound; the farts aren't from flatulence but from gulping air at the surface and storing it in their swim bladder.

Quiz 14

1) Based on oxygen usage, what animal is the most efficient swimmer?

2) Which of the basic tastes can't cats taste?

3) How many eyes do bees have?

4) Relative to its own weight, what is the strongest organism known?

5) Why is horseshoe crab blood worth $14,000 per quart?

6) What mammal needs the least sleep?

7) What blood type do mosquitoes like most?

8) What species of animal (not microscopic) has the largest size difference between males and females?

9) Excluding man, what animal species has the longest tested memory?

10) Research has shown that most mammals on average live for about the same number of heartbeats; how many?

Quiz 14 Answers

1) Jellyfish – It uses 48% less oxygen than any other known animal; they never stop moving.

2) Sweet – They don't have taste receptors for sweet; this applies to all cats domestic and wild.

3) Five

4) Gonorrhea bacterium – They can pull with a force of 100,000 times their body weight which is comparable to a 150-pound person pulling 7,500 tons.

5) Its unique chemical properties make it very valuable in the health care industry for bacterial testing. It can coagulate around as little as one part in a trillion of bacterial contamination, and the reaction only takes forty-five minutes instead of two days with mammalian blood.

6) Giraffes – They only sleep 30 minutes a day on average just a few

minutes at a time.

7) Type O

8) Blanket octopus – Females are 10,000 to 40,000 times larger than males; females may be 6.5 feet in length; males are 1 inch.

9) Dolphins – Bottlenose dolphins have unique whistles like names; studies have shown that they remember the whistle of other dolphins they have lived with even after 20 years of separation.

10) 1.5 billion – Larger animals have slower heartbeats, so they live longer; humans used to fit the pattern prior to health and medical improvements.

Quiz 15

1) What land mammal has the most teeth?

2) What land animal has the most teeth?

3) Some snakes, Komodo dragons, sharks, and turkeys are all capable of what biblical feat?

4) What female mammal can literally die if she doesn't mate?

5) What is a group of owls called?

6) What was the first domesticated animal?

7) Humans only have 1, but leeches have 32 what?

8) What is a group of cats called?

9) What bird can only eat when its head is upside down?

10) What is the only creature that can turn its stomach inside out?

Quiz 15 Answers

1) Opossum – 50

2) Giant armadillo – up to 100

3) Virgin births

4) Ferret – The female stays in heat until she mates; if she doesn't, very high levels of estrogen remain in her blood for a long time and can cause aplastic anemia and death. She doesn't have to get pregnant, but she must mate.

5) Parliament

6) Dog

7) Brains – Each controls a different segment of their body.

8) Clowder
9) Flamingo
10) Starfish

Quiz 16

1) What animal has the largest eye?
2) An elephant has 40,000 what in its trunk?
3) What animal produces its own sunscreen?
4) In ancient China, what dog breed was restricted to the aristocracy?
5) What insect may be the most efficient predator and possibly has the best vision of any animal?
6) What animal always gives birth to four identical offspring?
7) The nine-banded armadillo and humans have what in common?
8) The minnow is the smallest member of what fish family?
9) Based on AKC registrations, what are the three most popular purebred dog breeds in the U.S.?
10) What land mammal has the best sense of smell?

Quiz 16 Answers

1) Giant and colossal squid - up to 11-inch diameter
2) Muscles – Humans only have about 650 muscles in their entire body.
3) Hippopotamus – They produce a mucus like secretion that keeps them cool and acts as a powerful sunscreen.
4) Pekingese
5) Dragonfly - Humans have three light sensitive proteins in the eye for red, blue, and green (tri-chromatic vision); dragonflies have up to 33. Their bulbous eyes have 30,000 facets and can see in all directions at once. Studies have also shown that they catch as much as 95% of their intended prey.
6) Armadillo - A single embryo splits into four as part of their normal reproduction.
7) Leprosy – They are the only animals known to be infected.
8) Carp or cyprinid
9) Labrador Retrievers, German Shepherds, Golden Retrievers

10) Bear – Black bears have been observed to travel 18 miles in a straight line to a food source; grizzlies can find an elk carcass underwater, and polar bears can smell a seal through 3 feet of ice.

Quiz 17

1) A horse's height is measured from the ground to what part?

2) What would happen to you if you ate a polar bear's liver?

3) A newborn Bactrian camel has how many humps?

4) What biological aspect of a mouse is bigger than an elephant's?

5) What animal has the highest blood pressure?

6) What is the only native North American marsupial?

7) The ostrich is the largest bird in the world; what is the second largest?

8) How many compartments does a cow's stomach have?

9) **What is the longest living land mammal after man?**

10) What is the longest living land animal of any kind?

Quiz 17 Answers

1) Withers - base of the neck above the shoulders

2) You would get vitamin A poisoning and could die. Polar bears have 50-60 times normal human levels of vitamin A in their liver, and it is about 3 times the tolerable level that a human can intake.

3) None - Baby camels don't get their humps until they start eating solid food.

4) Sperm - Large animals tend to have high numbers of smaller sperm.

5) Giraffe – about 300 over 200

6) Opossum

7) Southern cassowary – It lives in the tropical rainforests of Indonesia, New Guinea, and the islands of northern Australia and averages about 100 pounds compared to 230 pounds for the ostrich.

8) Four

9) Elephant – up to 86 years

10) Tortoise – up to 250 years

Quiz 18

1) Where are a snail's reproductive organs?
2) What is a newly hatched swan called?
3) How many rows of whiskers does a cat have?
4) What resin used in varnish is a secretion of an insect?
5) What is the largest cat in the Americas?
6) What fish's skin was once used commercially as sandpaper?
7) Which leg of a chicken is more tender, left or right leg?
8) What can't rats do that makes them particularly vulnerable to poison?
9) What does the horned toad squirt from its eyes when attacked?
10) The cheetah is the fastest land animal; what is the second fastest?

Quiz 18 Answers

1) Head
2) Cygnet
3) Four
4) Shellac – lac insect
5) Jaguar – It is the third largest cat after the tiger and lion.
6) Shark
7) Left leg – Chickens scratch with their right leg building up more muscle in that leg and making it tougher than the left.
8) Vomit
9) Blood
10) Pronghorn antelope – 55 mph

Quiz 19

1) What bird has the biggest brain relative to its body size?
2) What was the first bird domesticated by man?
3) For animals, what is the summer equivalent to hibernation?
4) How many claws does a normal house cat have?
5) What is the only known animal to regularly prey on adult bears?
6) How many hearts does an octopus have?

7) What is the only dog breed specifically mentioned in the Bible?

8) What color is a polar bear's fur?

9) Napoleon's life was saved by what breed of dog?

10) A cat is feline; what kind of animal is leporine?

Quiz 19 Answers

1) Hummingbird – over 4% of its body weight

2) Goose

3) Estivation – Animals slow their activity for the hot, dry summer months.

4) 18 – five on each front paw and four on each back paw

5) Tiger

6) Three

7) Greyhound

8) It has no color; it is transparent and appears white only because it reflects visible light.

9) Newfoundland – It saved him from drowning.

10) Rabbit

Quiz 20

1) Where are a cricket's ears located?
2) What order of insects contains the most species?
3) What species of whale dives deeper and stays underwater the longest?
4) What is a group of rattlesnakes called?
5) What is the closest living relative to the **Tyrannosaurus Rex**?
6) Silkworms live on a diet of leaves from only what plant?
7) What was the penalty in ancient Egypt for killing a cat even accidentally?
8) Dalmatian dogs originated in what country?
9) What is the only land mammal native to New Zealand?
10) Humans and what two other species of animals are the only ones to go through menopause?

Quiz 20 Answers

1) Front legs
2) Beetles
3) Sperm whale – They can dive for more than an hour and more than 4,000 feet deep.
4) A rhumba
5) Chicken
6) Mulberry
7) Death
8) Croatia – Dalmatia region
9) Bat
10) Killer whales and short finned pilot whales

Arts

Quiz 1

1) What did Sheryl Crow do before she became a singer?
2) What drink did Johann Sebastian Bach enjoy so much that he wrote a cantata for it?
3) In the song "My Darling Clementine", how did Clementine die?
4) What modern musical instrument evolved from the sackbut?
5) What painter's work is the most stolen?
6) What group sang "Wild Thing" in 1966?
7) What was the first compact disc recording released in the U.S.?
8) What painting depicts the sister and dentist of artist Grant Wood?
9) Victor Willis, Felipe Rose, Randy Jones, David Hodo, Glenn Hughes, and Alex Briley are all members of what singing group?
10) What singer did Elvis Presley say was the greatest in the world?

Quiz 1 Answers

1) Teacher
2) Coffee
3) Drowned
4) Trombone
5) Pablo Picasso
6) Troggs
7) *Born in the USA*
8) *American Gothic*
9) The Village People
10) Roy Orbison

Quiz 2

1) Who was the lead singer of Herman's Hermits?
2) What singer was married to Debbie Reynolds, Elizabeth Taylor, and Connie Stevens?

3) How many paintings did Vincent Van Gogh sell while he was alive?

4) What duo had a hit with the song "Islands in the Stream"?

5) What musical features the song "Getting to Know You"?

6) What instrument did Bob Dylan play in his recording debut?

7) What natural landmark was the inspiration for the song "America the Beautiful"?

8) What is the barber of Seville's name?

9) What was Chuck Berry's only number one hit?

10) What was the biggest hit for The Animals in 1964?

Quiz 2 Answers

1) Peter Noone

2) Eddie Fisher

3) One

4) Kenny Rogers and Dolly Parton

5) *The King and I*

6) Harmonica

7) Pikes Peak

8) Figaro

9) "My Ding-a-ling"

10) "House of the Rising Sun"

Quiz 3

1) How many movements traditionally make up a concerto?

2) Who is the youngest solo singer ever to win a Grammy?

3) What was Buddy Holly's first hit single?

4) John Henry Deutchendorf became famous under what name?

5) What act has the most Billboard Hot 100 entries of all time?

6) In Greek mythology, how many heads did the Hydra have?

7) Who wrote the music for *Showboat*?

8) Who wrote the symphonic fairy tale *Peter and the Wolf*?

9) Who wrote the song "I Will Always Love You"?

10) In what method of singing does the singer alternate between

natural voice and falsetto?

Quiz 3 Answers

1) Three
2) Leann Rimes – 13
3) "That'll Be the Day"
4) John Denver
5) Glee cast – 207
6) Nine
7) Jerome Kern
8) Sergei Prokofiev
9) Dolly Parton
10) Yodeling

Quiz 4

1) What is Frank Sinatra's middle name?
2) Whose son flew too close to the Sun on waxen wings?
3) What 1958 song was The Coaster's only number one hit?
4) Who is generally given credit for coining the term "rock and roll"?
5) In Greek mythology, who was the first woman on Earth?
6) The Passion Play is performed every 10 years where?
7) Who recorded "King of the Road" in 1965?
8) In Greek mythology, who solved the riddle of the Sphinx?
9) Who was a founder and first director of the New York City Ballet?
10) Who is Hercules' father?

Quiz 4 Answers

1) Albert
2) Daedalus
3) "Yakety Yak"
4) Alan Freed
5) Pandora
6) Oberammergau, Germany

7) Roger Miller
8) Oedipus
9) George Balanchine
10) Zeus

Quiz 5

1) The Dove Awards are presented annually for what?
2) Who painted *The Water Lilly Pond* in 1899?
3) What are the names of The Three Tenors?
4) What is the world's best-selling musical instrument?
5) In Greek mythology, what did Daedalus construct for Minos?
6) Who was the first woman inducted into the Country Music Hall of Fame in 1973?
7) Who was the first woman inducted into the Rock and Roll Hall of Fame in 1987?
8) In Greek mythology, who gave fire to mankind?
9) What 1960s protest song includes the line "Think of all the hate there is in Red China, then take a look around to Selma, Alabama"?
10) From what musical does the song "On the Street Where You Live" come?

Quiz 5 Answers

1) Gospel music
2) Claude Monet
3) Jose Carreras, Placido Domingo, Luciano Pavarotti
4) Harmonica
5) Labyrinth
6) Patsy Cline
7) Aretha Franklin
8) Prometheus
9) "Eve of Destruction" – Barry McGuire
10) *My Fair Lady*

Quiz 6

1) Who wrote the opera *Rigoletto*?
2) What are the four sections of an orchestra?
3) What is painting in water color on fresh plaster called?
4) What famous religious hymn was composed by Augustus Montague Toplady in the 18th century?
5) In Greek mythology, who ferries the dead across the river Styx?
6) Who composed *Appalachian Spring*?
7) What singer's autobiography is titled *Bound for Glory*?
8) What was the number one song of the 1970s in the U.S.?
9) What musical features the song "Old Man River"?
10) In Arthurian legend, who is Lancelot's son?

Quiz 6 Answers

1) Giuseppe Verdi
2) Strings, wood wind, brass, percussion
3) Fresco
4) "Rock of Ages"
5) Charon
6) Aaron Copeland
7) Woody Guthrie
8) "You Light Up My Life" – Debby Boone
9) *Showboat*
10) Galahad

Quiz 7

1) What classical composer wrote "Hark the Herald Angels Sing"?
2) Who was Bette Midler's piano player before he went solo?
3) What song was originally "Good Morning to All" before the words were changed, and it was published in 1935?
4) Who was part of the Million Dollar Quartet in an informal 1956 recording?
5) Who was condemned in Hades to forever push a boulder uphill,

only for it to come rolling down before it reached the top?

6) Who sang "Monster Mash"?

7) What sixth century Greek poet is the father of drama?

8) In 1981, who won song of the year with "Sailing"?

9) What band was named after the inventor of the seed drill?

10) What actor was the narrator on Michael Jackson's *Thriller*?

Quiz 7 Answers

1) Felix Mendelssohn

2) Barry Manilow

3) "Happy Birthday to You"

4) Elvis Presley, Jerry Lee Lewis, Carl Perkins, Johnny Cash

5) Sisyphus

6) Bobby Boris Picket and the Crypt Kickers

7) Thespis

8) Christopher Cross

9) Jethro Tull

10) Vincent Price

Quiz 8

1) What group originally sang "Louie Louie"?

2) Who wrote *La Traviata*?

3) What renaissance artist had the surname Buonarroti?

4) Who wrote *The Flight of the Bumblebee*?

5) In what musical is the song "Hey Big Spender" featured?

6) In music, what is a semihemidemisemiquaver?

7) According to Wurlitzer, what is the most popular jukebox song of all time?

8) What famous artist could write with both his left and right hand simultaneously?

9) What do the initials B.B. stand for in B.B. King's name?

10) "Ebony and Ivory" was a hit for what famous duo?

Quiz 8 Answers

1) The Kingsmen
2) Giuseppe Verdi
3) Michelangelo
4) Nicolai Rimsky Korsakov
5) *Sweet Charity*
6) 1/128th note
7) "Hound Dog" – Elvis Presley
8) Leonardo da Vinci
9) Blues Boy
10) Paul McCartney and Stevie Wonder

Quiz 9

1) Who has performed more concerts in Madison Square garden than any other artist?
2) What female singer died of alcohol poisoning in 2011 at the age of 27?
3) Who wrote and recorded "Spirit in the Sky"?
4) What singer wrote and first recorded "Blue Suede Shoes"?
5) In the song "Yankee Doodle", what does the term macaroni mean?
6) How many copies must an album sell to be certified diamond?
7) Who had the number one song "The Battle of New Orleans"?
8) What is the name of the Greek goddess of victory?
9) Who is the best-selling Canadian singer of all time?
10) What famous musician was fatally shot by his father in 1984?

Quiz 9 Answers

1) Elton John
2) Amy Winehouse
3) Norman Greenbaum
4) Carl Perkins
5) Stylish or fashionable – In late 18th century England, macaroni meant stylish or fashionable; in the song, it is used to mock the

Americans who think they can be stylish by simply sticking a feather in their cap.

6) 10 million
7) Johnny Horton
8) Nike
9) Celine Dion
10) Marvin Gaye

Quiz 10

1) What was the highest selling album of the 1980s in the U.S.?
2) What is the Roman name for the goddess Hecate?
3) What Broadway show has the longest run in history?
4) What famous artist was struck in the face by a rival and disfigured for life?
5) Who has the most all-time number one hits on Billboard's Hot 100?
6) What artist had the first record to sell over 1 million copies?
7) Based on decibels, what is the loudest instrument in a standard orchestra?
8) How many people have won all four major American entertainment awards (Oscar, Emmy, Tony, Grammy)?
9) Who has won the most Grammy Awards?
10) Who is the youngest artist to win an album of the year Grammy?

Quiz 10 Answers

1) *Thriller* - Michael Jackson
2) Trivia
3) *Phantom of the Opera*
4) Michelangelo
5) Beatles – 20
6) Enrico Caruso – 1902
7) Trombone – about 115 decibels
8) 15 – Richard Rogers, Helen Hayes, Rita Moreno, John Gielgud, Audrey Hepburn, Marvin Hamlisch, Mel Brooks, Whoopi Goldberg, Jonathan Tunick, Mike Nichols, Scott Rudin, Robert Lopez, John Legend, Tim Rice, Andrew Lloyd Weber

9) George Solti – 31
10) Taylor Swift – 20

Quiz 11

1) Who wrote and sang "Hello Muddah, Hello Fadduh" about Camp Granada?
2) Who composed *Pomp and Circumstance*?
3) In Greek mythology, who gave Midas the power to turn everything to gold?
4) Who wrote the music *Ride of the Valkyries*?
5) What is the lowest female singing voice called?
6) "I Don't Know How to Love Him" is from what musical?
7) Carlos Marin, Urs Buhler, Sebastien Izambard, and David Miller are members of what vocal group?
8) The Greek statue *Discobolus* is better known by what name?
9) Who composed *The Four Seasons*?
10) Who is the oldest artist to have a number one hit on Billboard's Hot 100?

Quiz 11 Answers

1) Allan Sherman
2) Edward Elgar
3) Dionysus
4) Richard Wagner
5) Contralto
6) *Jesus Christ Superstar*
7) Il Divo
8) *The Discus Thrower*
9) Antonio Vivaldi
10) Louis Armstrong – 62 with "Hello Dolly" in 1964

Quiz 12

1) Who is the oldest female artist to have a number one hit on Billboard's Hot 100?

2) Who is the youngest solo artist to have a number one hit on Billboard's Hot 100?

3) Who is the oldest living artist to have a song on Billboard's Hot 100?

4) What songwriter has the most number one singles on Billboard's Hot 100?

5) What artist has the most consecutive number one singles on Billboard's Hot 100?

6) What song has the most weeks at number one ever for an instrumental?

7) Janis Joplin, Jimi Hendrix, and Kurt Cobain all died at what age?

8) What singing duo started out as Caesar and Cleo?

9) What is the name of the last Beatles album recorded before they split up?

10) What is the highest male singing voice called?

Quiz 12 Answers

1) Cher – 52 in 1999

2) Stevie Wonder – 13 with "Fingertips Part 2" in 1963

3) Tony Bennet – 85 in 2011

4) Paul McCartney

5) Whitney Houston – seven

6) "Theme from a Summer Place" – nine weeks in 1960

7) 27

8) Sonny and Cher

9) *Abbey Road*

10) Countertenor

Quiz 13

1) What country has the highest number of museums per capita?

2) The blood red sky in Edvard Munch's famous painting *The Scream* is believed to be due to what rather than the artist's imagination?

3) Where was the largest free rock concert ever held?

4) Early in his career, Picasso was so poor he did what with most of his early work?

5) Who said, "I think, therefore I am"?

6) Who are the only two people ever to win an Oscar, Emmy, Tony, Grammy, and Pulitzer?

7) In 1939, Earl Wild was the first pianist to give a recital on U.S. television; in 1997, he was also the first person to do what?

8) How many of his own songs did Elvis Presley write?

9) What music group used to be called Johnny and the Moondogs?

10) What is the first and only music group to play on all seven continents?

Quiz 13 Answers

1) Israel

2) Krakatoa eruption in 1883 – The dust and gases from the eruption caused fiery sunrises and sunsets in Norway that Munch witnessed.

3) Rio de Janeiro, Brazil – Rod Stewart played to 4.2 million people on Copacabana Beach on New Year's Eve 1994.

4) He burned them to keep his apartment warm.

5) Rene Descartes – philosopher, mathematician, scientist, father of analytical geometry

6) Richard Rogers and Marvin Hamlisch

7) Stream a piano performance over the internet

8) None

9) Beatles

10) Metallica

Quiz 14

1) Whose music does the British navy play to help scare off Somali pirates?

2) What country has the highest number of heavy metal bands per capita?

3) Who had the only number one song recorded by a father and daughter?

4) Who is the only person ever to win a Nobel Prize, Pulitzer, Oscar, and Grammy?

5) What does the word ukulele literally mean?

6) What classical composer wrote numerous letters and an entire song focused on poop?

7) What year was the first piano made?

8) Mozart and Beethoven composed music for the glass armonica instrument; who invented it?

9) What kind of paint did Picasso use?

10) Elvis Presley won three Grammy awards; what music category were his three wins?

Quiz 14 Answers

1) Britney Spears

2) Finland

3) Frank and Nancy Sinatra – "Something Stupid" in 1967

4) Bob Dylan

5) Jumping flea – likely after the movements of the player's fingers

6) Mozart – No one is sure if it was his odd humor or a mental issue.

7) 1698

8) Benjamin Franklin – It replicated the sound a wet finger makes when rubbed along the rim of a glass and became very popular.

9) House paint

10) Gospel – His earliest work was before the Grammys started in 1958.

Quiz 15

1) Carl and the Passions changed their band name to what?

2) Whose band was the Quarrymen?

3) In the song "Waltzing Matilda", what is a jumbuck?

4) Who had a hit with the song "Loco-Motion" in 1962?

5) La Giaconda is better known as what?

6) Who wrote the opera Madam Butterfly?

7) Robert Allen Zimmerman is the real name of what music artist?

8) The Aphrodite of Melos has what better known name?

9) On what is the Mona Lisa painted?

10) The band The Detours changed their name to The High Numbers

and then what name?

Quiz 15 Answers

1) Beach Boys
2) John Lennon – The band evolved into the Beatles.
3) Sheep
4) Little Eva
5) *Mona Lisa*
6) Giacomo Puccini
7) Bob Dylan
8) *Venus de Milo*
9) Wood – thin poplar panel
10) The Who

Quiz 16

1) What Henry Mancini song won an Oscar and a Grammy?
2) Who is the only artist to win best new artist and record, album, and song of the year Grammys in the same year?
3) What opera is about a female cigarette factory worker?
4) Composer Vivaldi had what other profession?
5) Tempera paint's primary ingredients are water and what?
6) Beethoven, Brahms, Chopin, Handel, Liszt, and Ravel have what in common in their personal lives?
7) "What I Did for Love" is from what Broadway musical?
8) Who wrote the song "Johnny B. Goode"?
9) What town is the setting for *The Music Man*?
10) What Italian artist painted *Birth of Venus*?

Quiz 16 Answers

1) "Moon River" – *Breakfast at Tiffany's* Oscar
2) Christopher Cross – 1981
3) *Carmen*
4) Priest
5) Egg yolk

6) Bachelors
7) *A Chorus Line*
8) Chuck Berry
9) River City
10) Sandro Botticelli

Quiz 17

1) What had one eye, one horn, and flew in Sheb Wooley's 1958 hit?
2) Who originally sang "Johnny Angel"?
3) Who was the oldest member of the Beatles?
4) What was Rembrandt's last name?
5) Who wrote more than 1,000 songs including "This Land is Your Land"?
6) Who replaced Pete Best?
7) What Broadway show introduced the song "Some Enchanted Evening"?
8) What Broadway musical was inspired by *Don Quixote*?
9) What comedian had the first comedy album ever to hit number one?
10) What Gilbert and Sullivan opera is about the emperor of Japan?

Quiz 17 Answers

1) Flying Purple People Eater
2) Shelley Fabares
3) Ringo Starr
4) Van Rijn
5) Woody Guthrie
6) Ringo Starr – He took his place in the Beatles in 1962.
7) *South Pacific*
8) *Man of La Mancha*
9) Bob Newhart – *The Button-Down Mind of Bob Newhart* in 1960
10) *The Mikado*

Quiz 18

1) Who jumped off the Tallahatchie Bridge?
2) What is the only single by the same artist to go to number one twice?
3) In Greek mythology, what beautiful youth pined for the love of his reflection?
4) What was the last Rogers and Hammerstein musical?
5) Who wrote the song "God Bless America"?
6) Who is the fourth person mentioned in Dion DiMucci's song "Abraham, Martin and John"?
7) Who wrote "Rhapsody in Blue"?
8) What 1966 hit was sung by Sergeant Barry Sadler?
9) Who painted *The Blue Boy*?
10) Who is the principal character in *Fiddler on the Roof*?

Quiz 18 Answers

1) Billy Joe McAllister
2) "The Twist" – Chubby Checker in 1960 and 1961
3) Narcissus
4) *The Sound of Music*
5) Irving Berlin
6) Bobby Kennedy
7) George Gershwin
8) "The Ballad of the Green Berets"
9) Thomas Gainsborough
10) Tevye

Quiz 19

1) What is the longest (minutes of play time) song to ever reach number one on the Billboard Hot 100?
2) An orchestra usually tunes up to what instrument?
3) What is the only band to play at both Woodstock and Live Aid?
4) What German composer married the daughter of Franz Liszt?

5) Who was the top selling recording artist in the U.S. in the 1990s?

6) In Norse mythology, what is the name of the ultimate battle?

7) In *Peter and the Wolf*, what instrument represents the cat?

8) In Scandinavian mythology, what bridge links Heaven and Earth?

9) Who received the first ever music gold disc?

10) When the *Mona Lisa* was stolen from the Louvre in 1911, what famous artist was questioned as a suspect?

Quiz 19 Answers

1) "American Pie" by Don McLean – The original version ran for 8 minutes and 38 seconds.

2) Oboe

3) The Who

4) Richard Wagner

5) Garth Brooks – more than 45 million albums in the 1990s

6) Ragnarok

7) Clarinet

8) Bifrost

9) Glenn Miller – "Chattanooga Choo Choo" in 1942

10) Pablo Picasso

History

Quiz 1

1) Alexander the Great was king of what country?
2) What year did Ferdinand Magellan complete the first circumnavigation of the world?
3) In what country were Arabic numerals first used?
4) Who made the first solo round the world flight?
5) What U.S. founding father was carried to the Constitutional Convention in a sedan chair carried by prisoners?
6) Who succeeded Adolf Hitler in 1945 as leader of Germany?
7) Who was the first honorary U.S. citizen?
8) Who was Temujin better known as?
9) Who was *Time* magazine's 1938 man of the year?
10) What queen married two of her brothers?

Quiz 1 Answers

1) Macedonia
2) 1522
3) India
4) Wiley Post – 1933
5) Benjamin Franklin
6) Admiral Karl Donitz
7) Winston Churchill
8) Genghis Khan
9) Adolf Hitler
10) Cleopatra

Quiz 2

1) Good King Wenceslas was king of what country?
2) The spire on the Empire State building was meant to be used for what?

3) What year did the Berlin wall fall?

4) Who was the first African American in space?

5) Who was the first man to set foot on all the continents other than Antarctica?

6) During the War of 1812, British troops invaded and burned what U.S. landmark?

7) What year was the first telephone call made?

8) What year did the Volkswagen Beetle make its first appearance?

9) Who was the first British monarch to visit America?

10) Who taught Alexander the Great?

Quiz 2 Answers

1) Bohemia – current Czech Republic

2) Airship dock

3) 1989

4) Guion Bluford

5) Captain James Cook

6) White House

7) 1876

8) 1938

9) George VI – 1939

10) Aristotle

Quiz 3

1) What year was the first U.S. minimum wage instituted?

2) What year did India gain independence from British colonial rule?

3) What book was given to all officers in the Confederate army during the U.S. Civil War?

4) What civilization first domesticated guinea pigs and used them for food, sacrifices, and household pets?

5) Through what town did Lady Godiva ride naked?

6) Who was outlaw Harry Longabaugh better known as?

7) What country did Abel Tasman discover in 1642?

8) By what name is Princess Sophia of Anhalt-Zerbst better known?

9) What country invented the crossbow?

10) Who ordered the Russian nobility to become more European by shaving off their beards?

Quiz 3 Answers

1) 1938 – 25 cents per hour

2) 1947

3) Les Misérables – Robert E. Lee believed the book symbolized their cause.

4) Incas

5) Coventry, England

6) Sundance Kid

7) New Zealand

8) Catherine the Great

9) China – about 700 BC

10) Peter the Great

Quiz 4

1) What was the profession of serial killer Ted Bundy?

2) What nationality was the first person in space who wasn't American or Russian?

3) What was the name of Alexander the Great's horse?

4) Who was Abraham Lincoln's first choice to lead the Union army?

5) What was Lech Walesa's job before he founded Solidarity?

6) Where was the first U.S. federal penitentiary?

7) British King Edward VIII abdicated his throne to marry who?

8) Who discovered the source of the Nile River?

9) What Roman killed himself after his defeat at Actium?

10) How many years were there between the first female in space and the first American female in space?

Quiz 4 Answers

1) Attorney

2) Czech – Vladimir Remek in 1978

3) Bucephalus

4) Robert E. Lee

5) Electrician

6) Leavenworth, Kansas

7) Wallis Simpson

8) John Hanning Speke

9) Mark Antony

10) 20 years – A Soviet woman was the first in 1963.

Quiz 5

1) The saying "Don't give up the ship!" comes from the last words of Captain James Lawrence in what war?

2) What is widely considered "The Gun that Won the West"?

3) What explorer visited Australia and New Zealand and surveyed the Pacific coast of North America?

4) What did the Romans call the tenth part of a legion?

5) What is the oldest alcoholic beverage to gain widespread popularity?

6) Why was the Eiffel Tower built?

7) What year did U.S. prohibition come to an end?

8) What explorer's last words were "I have not told half of what I saw"?

9) What year was NASA founded?

10) What famous battle took place July 1 to July 3, 1863?

Quiz 5 Answers

1) War of 1812

2) Winchester Model 1873 rifle

3) Captain George Vancouver

4) Cohort - 300 to 600 men

5) Mead – about 2000 BC from fermenting honey

6) Celebrate the 100th anniversary of the French Revolution

7) 1933

8) Marco Polo

9) 1958

10) Gettysburg

Quiz 6

1) What was the real name of the Boston Strangler?

2) Who is known as the father of modern economics?

3) How long was Nelson Mandela in prison?

4) Who was King of Mycenae and commander of the Greek forces in the Trojan War?

5) What did Albert Einstein call "the hardest thing in the world to understand"?

6) Who was the first American born child of English settlers?

7) Who is known as the father of medicine?

8) Introduced in 1888, the first vending machine in the U.S. dispensed what item?

9) Fylfot is a heraldic name for what symbol?

10) The U.S. icon Uncle Sam is based on Samuel Wilson who did what during the War of 1812?

Quiz 6 Answers

1) Albert DeSalvo

2) Adam Smith

3) 27 years

4) Agamemnon

5) Income taxes

6) Virginia Dare

7) Hippocrates

8) Gum

9) Swastika

10) Meat packer – He supplied barrels of beef to the army stamped with "U.S." for United States, but soldiers started referring to it as Uncle Sam's.

Quiz 7

1) What religion was Adolf Hitler?

2) What is the real name of the serial killer known as Son of Sam?

3) When was apartheid introduced in South Africa?

4) What was the family name of the French brothers who were pioneers in hot air ballooning and conducted the first untethered flights?

5) What year did the U.S. celebrate its sesquicentennial?

6) Who did Adolf Hitler dictate *Mein Kampf* to while in prison?

7) Who was the first Christian emperor of Rome?

8) Who first suggested the idea of daylight saving time in an essay he wrote in 1784?

9) What happened July 15, 1815 on the *HMS Bellerophon*?

10) What was the name given to textile workers who opposed modernization during the 19th century?

Quiz 7 Answers

1) Roman Catholic

2) David Berkowitz

3) 1948

4) Montgolfier

5) 1926 – 150-year anniversary

6) Rudolf Hess

7) Constantine the Great - emperor from 306 to 337

8) Benjamin Franklin

9) Napoleon surrendered

10) Luddites

Quiz 8

1) On December 1, 1917, who opened Boys Town, a farm village for wayward boys, near Omaha, Nebraska?

2) Who assassinated John Lennon?

3) Where did Churchill, Roosevelt and Stalin meet in 1945?

4) Who was known as the father of the atomic bomb?

5) *Sputnik 2* was launched into space in 1957; what was the name of the dog that was on board?

6) At the battle of Actium, who defeated Mark Antony and Cleopatra?

7) What country's troops sustained the greatest number of deaths in WWII?

8) In the 15th century, what was the war between the houses of Lancaster and York?

9) What is the most visited paid monument in the world?

10) *The Ladies' Mercury* in 1693 was the world's first what?

Quiz 8 Answers

1) Father Edward Flanagan

2) Mark David Chapman

3) Yalta

4) Robert Oppenheimer

5) Laika

6) Octavian or Emperor Augustus

7) Soviet Union

8) War of the Roses

9) Eiffel Tower

10) Periodical designed and published for women

Quiz 9

1) What was the first lighthouse?

2) Who made the first phone call to the Moon?

3) What battle was fought at Senlac Hill?

4) In 1917, Janette Rankin become the first woman in the U.S. to do what?

5) What is the oldest college in the U.S.?

6) Who was the last English king to die on the battlefield?

7) What is the most powerful Earthbound explosion ever witnessed by humans?

8) What was the name of Robert E. Lee's horse?

9) What disease is believed to have killed more people than any other throughout history?

10) What year did the *Titanic* sink?

Quiz 9 Answers

1) Pharos of Alexandria – 280 BC

2) Richard Nixon

3) Battle of Hastings

4) Elected to the U.S. Congress

5) Harvard – 1636

6) Richard III

7) Mount Tambora volcanic eruption in 1815 in Indonesia – The explosion was equivalent to 800 megatons of TNT, 14 times larger than the largest man-made explosion.

8) Traveller

9) Malaria – Over 1 million people still die from malaria annually.

10) 1912

Quiz 10

1) Who was the first American astronaut who wasn't in the military when they went into space?

2) What political cartoonist popularized the use of the elephant and donkey as symbols of the two main U.S. political parties?

3) What was the first U.S. state to secede from the Union on December 20, 1860?

4) The Statue of Liberty originally also served what functional role?

5) In honor of whose death in 1931 were all non-essential lights in the U.S. turned off for one minute?

6) What American statesman wrote the collection of essays *Fart Proudly*?

7) Who was the first person to enter space (100 km above the Earth) twice?

8) How many states joined the Confederate States of America?

9) In the 16th century, King James IV of Scotland paid people to practice what on them?

10) Who was married to Adolf Hitler for one day?

Quiz 10 Answers

1) Neil Armstrong - He had been a Navy fighter pilot but was a

civilian when he joined NASA.

2) Thomas Nast

3) South Carolina

4) Lighthouse

5) Thomas Edison

6) Benjamin Franklin

7) Joseph A. Walker – X-15 rocket aircraft in 1963

8) 11

9) Dentistry – He was an amateur dentist and very interested in medicine; he established the Royal College of Surgeons in Scotland two centuries before it was established in England.

10) Eva Braun

Quiz 11

1) Opened in 1852, what infamous prison was off the coast of French Guiana?

2) What war did Joan of Arc's inspirational leadership help end?

3) What year did the first manned space flight occur?

4) The New Testament was originally written in what language?

5) What did Russian Valentina Tereshkova become the first woman to do in 1963?

6) In what war did jet fighter planes first battle each other?

7) According to legend, what historical figure died of a nosebleed on his wedding night?

8) The island of Krakatoa was almost entirely destroyed by a volcanic eruption in what year?

9) Who wrote the words that are engraved on the Statue of Liberty?

10) What city became the U.S. federal capital in 1789?

Quiz 11 Answers

1) Devil's Island

2) The Hundred Years War

3) 1961

4) Greek

5) Travel in space

6) Korean War

7) Attila the Hun

8) 1883

9) Emma Lazarus – The words were written in 1883 to raise money for the statue's pedestal.

10) New York

Quiz 12

1) What area of London did Jack the Ripper's murders occur in?

2) What famous priest ministered to the Molokai lepers from 1873 until his death?

3) What was the date for D-Day?

4) What was the last Chinese dynasty?

5) What was the predecessor to the United Nations?

6) How many witches were burned at the stake during the Salem witch trials?

7) Who was the first person to reach the South Pole in 1911?

8) What transportation route re-opened in 1975 after an eight-year closure?

9) What was discovered at Qumran in 1947?

10) What was the first ship to reach the *Titanic* after it sank?

Quiz 12 Answers

1) Whitechapel

2) Father Damien

3) June 6, 1944

4) Manchu

5) League of Nations

6) None - Twenty were executed, but most were hung, and none were burned.

7) Roald Amundsen

8) Suez Canal

9) Dead Sea Scrolls

10) *Carpathia*

Quiz 13

1) What year did Canada become a country?
2) Who was the first person to sail around the Cape of Good Hope?
3) Who was named *Time* magazine's Man of the Century in 1999?
4) How many states are needed to ratify an amendment to the U.S. Constitution?
5) Where was the tallest tsunami wave ever recorded?
6) Who assassinated Robert Kennedy?
7) Who was the first queen of England?
8) What is the only nation that created nuclear weapons and then voluntarily eliminated them?
9) What year did Cuba get its independence from the U.S.?
10) Who was the oldest person to sign the Declaration of Independence?

Quiz 13 Answers

1) 1867
2) Vasco da Gama
3) Albert Einstein
4) 38 – 75% of the states
5) Lituya Bay, Alaska in 1958 - An 8.0 earthquake dropped 40 to 50 million cubic yards of rock and ice 3,000 feet down into the bay creating a 1,720-foot wave.
6) Sirhan Sirhan
7) Mary I
8) South Africa
9) 1902
10) Benjamin Franklin – 70 at the time

Quiz 14

1) Less than a year before Abraham Lincoln was assassinated, who saved Lincoln's oldest son Robert from being hit by a train?
2) Tenochtitlan was the capital of what empire?

3) What U.S. Constitutional amendment granted women the right to vote?

4) What year was the Pledge of Allegiance written?

5) In what city did Rosa Parks refuse to give up her seat?

6) Where was the world's first underwater tunnel?

7) What was the first U.S. department store?

8) Who organized the Boston Tea Party?

9) Who is the only person to win two unshared Nobel Prizes?

10) What did Robert Heft design in 1958 as a part of a junior high history class project?

Quiz 14 Answers

1) Edwin Booth – brother of John Wilkes Booth

2) Aztec

3) 19th

4) 1892

5) Montgomery, Alabama

6) Thames River, London – 1843

7) Macy's – 1858

8) Samuel Adams

9) Linus Pauling

10) Current 50-star United States flag

Quiz 15

1) What was the nickname for the *Hughes H-4 Hercules* aircraft that made a single flight in 1947?

2) What year did Switzerland last go to war with another country?

3) What country landed the first man-made object on the Moon?

4) What empire lasted from 1324 to 1922?

5) What country did Adolf Hitler describe as a pimple on the face of Europe?

6) The final link of the first U.S. transcontinental railway was completed in what state?

7) What year did Mexico get its independence from Spain?

8) What country has the oldest parliament in the world?

9) Who was the first *Time* magazine man of the year?

10) Israel was founded in what year?

Quiz 15 Answers

1) *Spruce Goose*

2) 1515

3) Soviet Union – *Luna* 2 in 1959

4) Ottoman or Turkish Empire

5) Switzerland – Hitler hated Switzerland and thought it had no right to exist; he had a planned invasion but never initiated it.

6) Utah

7) 1810

8) Iceland - 930

9) Charles Lindbergh – 1927

10) 1948

Quiz 16

1) What year did the gunfight at the O.K. Corral take place?

2) What year was the U.S. Constitution written?

3) What year was the last public execution in the U.S.?

4) What was the first Confederate state to be readmitted to the Union after the Civil War?

5) What was suffragette Susan B. Anthony talking about when she said, "I think it has done more to emancipate women than anything else in the world. It gives women a feeling of freedom and self-reliance"?

6) How many people have died outside the Earth's atmosphere?

7) What newspaper mistakenly ran the infamous "Dewey Defeats Truman" headline?

8) How many people have walked on the Moon?

9) Who was the last man to walk on the Moon?

10) What country was known to Europeans as Cathay from the 11th to the 16th century?

Quiz 16 Answers

1) 1881
2) 1787
3) 1936 – Kentucky
4) Tennessee
5) Bicycling
6) Three – *Soyuz 11* in 1971
7) *Chicago Daily Tribune*
8) 12
9) Eugene Cernan
10) China

Quiz 17

1) What year did the U.S. complete the Louisiana Purchase?
2) The end of the Pony Express line was in what western city?
3) What state was the first to elect a woman to the U.S. Congress?
4) What is the bloodiest single day of battle in U.S. history?
5) What was the first nation to have a female prime minister?
6) Who was the first woman to win a Nobel Prize?
7) Who is the only person to win *Time* magazine's person of the year three times?
8) In what city was Archduke Ferdinand killed?
9) What year did seat belts become mandatory in U.S. cars?
10) What Spanish explorer is credited with discovering the Mississippi River?

Quiz 17 Answers

1) 1803
2) Sacramento, California
3) Montana
4) Battle of Antietam in the Civil War - 22,000 dead, wounded, or missing
5) Sri Lanka – 1960

6) Marie Curie

7) Franklin D. Roosevelt

8) Sarajevo

9) 1968

10) Hernando de Soto

Quiz 18

1) What country first tried unsuccessfully to build the Panama Canal?

2) Who was the pilot in the first fatal airplane crash?

3) What African country was settled by Americans?

4) Before devoting his life to philosophy, what was Socrates' profession?

5) What is the world's oldest snack food?

6) What was the first U.S. college to confer degrees on women?

7) Who was the first female candidate for U.S. vice president on a major party ticket?

8) What was the first city to reach a population of 1 million people?

9) What famous general was attacked by rabbits and had to retreat?

10) Who was the first woman appointed to the U.S. Supreme Court?

Quiz 18 Answers

1) France

2) Orville Wright

3) Liberia

4) Mason or stone cutter

5) Pretzels – sixth century

6) Oberlin College – 1841

7) Geraldine Ferraro – 1984

8) Rome – 5 BC

9) Napoleon – In 1807, Napoleon had just signed the Treaty of Tilsit ending his war with Russia; to celebrate, he went on a rabbit hunt. Hundreds of rabbits had been gathered for the hunt in cages, but when they were released, they swarmed toward Napoleon and his men rather than running away. They swarmed Napoleon's legs and started climbing up; he was forced to retreat to his coach and

depart. Instead of wild rabbits, they had bought tame rabbits that weren't afraid of people and probably thought it was feeding time.

10) Sandra Day O'Connor – 1981

Quiz 19

1) Who was Germany's first female chancellor?
2) What was the first major war campaign fought entirely by air forces?
3) Who was the first American casualty of the Revolutionary War?
4) What U.S. Constitutional amendment ended slavery?
5) What country gained its independence from Denmark in 1944?
6) Kim Campbell was the first female prime minister of what country?
7) Who was the famous wife of Leofric Earl of Mercia?
8) In what century did Cleopatra rule Egypt?
9) What was the first man made object to break the sound barrier?
10) Who is the Danish explorer who gave his name to a strait, sea, island, glacier, and land bridge?

Quiz 19 Answers

1) Angela Merkel
2) Battle of Britain
3) Crispus Attucks
4) 13th
5) Iceland
6) Canada – June 25 to November 4, 1993
7) Lady Godiva
8) First century BC
9) Whip
10) Vitus Bering

Quiz 20

1) Who was the first female U.S. Attorney General?
2) Who is the head of state of New Zealand?
3) What world leader had the nickname "The Great Asparagus"?

4) Who reached the summit of Mount Everest with Edmund Hilary in 1953?

5) Who was the first man to hit a golf ball on the Moon?

6) What Mediterranean island gained its independence from Britain in 1960?

7) On taking power in 1959, Fidel Castro banned what board game and ordered all sets destroyed?

8) The 1964 Nobel Peace Prize was awarded to its youngest recipient up to that point; who was it?

9) The Statue of Liberty was originally intended for what country?

10) What year did London get back to its pre-WWII population?

Quiz 20 Answers

1) Janet Reno

2) Queen Elizabeth II

3) Charles de Gaulle – He got the name in military school because of his looks.

4) Tenzing Norgay – Sherpa

5) Alan Shepard

6) Cyprus

7) Monopoly – He viewed it as the embodiment of capitalism.

8) Martin Luther King Jr. – 35

9) Egypt – They rejected it.

10) 2015

Quiz 21

1) What is the longest war in U.S. history?

2) What is the loudest sound in recorded history?

3) The Egyptian pyramids were built by what kind of workers?

4) Before he assumed office, Pope Pius II wrote one of the most popular books of the 15th century; what kind of book was it?

5) Who had the largest volunteer army in world history?

6) How many times in history has a submerged submarine deliberately sunk a submerged submarine?

7) During a 10-day period in 2001, Argentina had how many

presidents?

8) Elena Cornaro Piscopia was the first woman in the world to receive a PhD degree in what year?

9) Roman gladiator fights started as a part of what ceremony?

10) From the middle ages until 1809, Finland was part of what country?

Quiz 21 Answers

1) Afghan War – started 2001

2) Eruption of Krakatoa in 1883 – It ruptured people's eardrums 40 miles away and was clearly heard 3,000 miles away.

3) Paid laborers – not slaves

4) Erotic novel – a tale of two lovers

5) India – 2.5 million during WWII

6) Once

7) Five – economic crash combined with defaulting on foreign debt

8) 1678 – Italy

9) Funerals – When wealthy nobles died, they would have bouts at the graveside.

10) Sweden

Quiz 22

1) What year was the first magazine launched?

2) In 1917, Germany invited what country to join WWI by attacking the U.S. to recover lost territories?

3) What was the first country to implement daylight saving time?

4) How long did it take Berlin to get back to its pre-WWII population?

5) What makes Graca Machel unique among first ladies of the world?

6) Who was the first Hispanic to serve on the U.S. Supreme Court?

7) What year was Antarctica first sighted?

8) Sheep grazed in New York's Central Park until what year?

9) How many Americans were killed in the Hiroshima atomic blast?

10) Of all the countries that celebrate an independence day, the largest number gained independence from what country?

Quiz 22 Answers

1) 1663 – German philosophy and literature magazine
2) Mexico
3) Germany – in 1916 to save energy in WWI
4) It still hasn't.
5) First lady of two separate countries – widow of Nelson Mandela (South Africa president) and Samora Machel (Mozambique president)
6) Sonia Sotomayor
7) 1820
8) 1934 – They were moved during the Great Depression for fear they would be eaten.
9) 12 – prisoners of war
10) Great Britain (58) - followed by France (26), Russia (21), Spain (21)

Quiz 23

1) Where were the remains of England's King Richard III found?
2) What is the world's oldest currency still in use?
3) What was the only independent South American country to send troops to fight in WWII?
4) The Eiffel Tower wasn't intended to be permanent; it was scheduled for demolition in 1909 but was saved to be used as what?
5) Prior to the 20th century in North America, what now popular and expensive food was considered a mark of poverty, used for fertilizer, and fed to slaves?
6) Why are there 60 seconds in a minute and 360 degrees in a circle?
7) Mississippi was the last state to officially ratify the 13th amendment abolishing slavery in what year?
8) Who was the last pharaoh of Egypt?
9) How many sides does the Great Pyramid of Giza have?
10) What year was the last man on the Moon?

Quiz 23 Answers

1) Buried under a parking lot in Leicester England in 2013. He died on the battlefield in 1485.

2) British pound – 1,200 years

3) Brazil

4) Radio tower

5) Lobster – Its reputation changed when modern transportation allowed shipping live lobsters to urban centers.

6) The ancient Babylonians did math in base 60 instead of base 10 and developed the concepts.

7) 2013 – Mississippi ratified the amendment in 1995 but didn't notify the U.S. archivist and didn't officially complete the process until 2013.

8) Cleopatra

9) Eight – Each of the four sides are split from base to tip by slight concave indentations.

10) 1972

Quiz 24

1) When the Persians were at war with the Egyptians, they rounded up and released as many of what animal as they could on the battlefield?

2) What two countries still haven't officially signed a peace treaty between them ending WWII?

3) Queen Elizabeth II served in what capacity in WWII?

4) Tsutomu Yamaguchi is the only recognized person in the world to survive what?

5) What country lost the greatest percentage of its population in WWII?

6) What was the only U.S. soil Japan occupied during WWII?

7) What year were the last German WWII POWs released from the Soviet Union?

8) Why did so many U.S. police departments adopt navy blue uniforms?

9) In what year was the first African American elected to serve in the U.S. Congress?

10) Louis Bonaparte, Napoleon's brother, was called the "King of Rabbits"; why?

Quiz 24 Answers

1) Cats – Knowing the Egyptians reverence for cats, they knew they would not want to do anything to hurt the cats; the Persians won.

2) Japan and Russia – dispute over the Kuril Islands

3) Mechanic and driver

4) Both Hiroshima and Nagasaki atomic blasts – He was in Hiroshima on business for the first bomb and then returned home to Nagasaki.

5) Poland – 20%

6) Aleutian Islands – two remote islands

7) 1956

8) They were surplus army uniforms from the Civil War.

9) 1870 – a senator from Mississippi and a representative from South Carolina

10) He mispronounced the Dutch phrase "I am your King," and instead said "I am your rabbit," when he took over rule of the Netherlands in 1806.

Quiz 25

1) Who is credited as being the first person to put wheels on an office chair?

2) Notre Dame Cathedral was almost demolished in the 19th century; what saved it?

3) How long did the Spanish Inquisition last?

4) Before unifying Italy, what was Giuseppe Garibaldi's occupation?

5) Alexander the Great, Julius Caesar, Genghis Khan, Napoleon, Mussolini and Hitler all suffered from ailurophobia; what is it?

6) Of the seven wonders of the ancient world, only the Great Pyramid of Giza still exists; which of the other seven wonders disappeared most recently?

7) Who was Europe's only Muslim king?

8) Who was the first person to fly across the English Channel?

9) In what war was "The Charge of the Light Brigade"?

10) Patty Hearst was kidnapped by what organization?

Quiz 25 Answers

1) Charles Darwin – 1840
2) Victor Hugo wrote *The Hunchback of Notre Dame* partially to save the cathedral from demolition.
3) 356 years – 1479 to 1834
4) Spaghetti salesman in Uruguay
5) Fear of cats
6) Lighthouse at Alexandria – It was toppled by earthquakes in the early 14th century, and its ruined stones were carried off by the late 15th century.
7) King Zog of Albania – coronated in 1928
8) Louis Bleriot
9) Crimean War
10) Symbionese Liberation Army (SLA)

Quiz 26

1) In what country were the Guns of Navarone installed?
2) What was discovered in 1922 by Howard Carter?
3) Who supposedly ran through the streets naked crying "Eureka!"?
4) Who sailed in the *Golden Hind*?
5) Where did the mutineers of the *Bounty* settle?
6) What links Brazil, Uruguay, Mozambique, and Angola?
7) In 1911, Hiram Bingham discovered what?
8) What Norwegian politician's name became synonymous with traitor?
9) In 1763, Great Britain traded Havana, Cuba to Spain for what?
10) Who did the U.S. buy the Virgin Islands from?

Quiz 26 Answers

1) Turkey
2) Tutankhamun's tomb
3) Archimedes
4) Sir Francis Drake

5) Pitcairn Islands

6) Portuguese colonies

7) Lost city of Machu Picchu

8) Vidkun Quisling

9) Florida

10) Denmark

Quiz 27

1) What country was the first to introduce old age pensions?

2) What country originated the concentration camp?

3) Other than the war itself, what killed an estimated 43,000 U.S. servicemen mobilized for WWI?

4) Why was Mary Mallon isolated from 1915 to 1938?

5) Who ran the first marathon upon which all others are based?

6) What is the oldest known name for the island of Great Britain?

7) In what month did the Russian October Revolution take place?

8) What country was the first to abolish capital punishment for all crimes?

9) Who was the original Peeping Tom looking at?

10) What did Lucien B. Smith invent in 1867 that had a great impact on the American west?

Quiz 27 Answers

1) Germany – 1889

2) Great Britain – during the Boer War

3) Influenza – about half of all U.S. military deaths in Europe

4) Typhoid Mary

5) Pheidippides - He ran 140 miles round trip from Athens to Sparta over mountainous terrain to ask for military aid; marched 26 miles from Athens to Marathon; fought all morning, and then ran 26 miles to Athens with the victory news and died of exhaustion.

6) Albion

7) November - It was October in the old Julian calendar.

8) Venezuela - by constitution in 1863

9) Lady Godiva

10) Barbed wire

Quiz 28

1) Who was offered the presidency of Israel in 1952 and turned it down?

2) In 1861, *The Times* newspaper of London carried the world's first what?

3) Edward Teach became famous as who?

4) What pet did Florence Nightingale carry with her?

5) Who is known as the father of history?

6) What did the ancient Greeks use instead of soap to clean themselves?

7) What country invented french fried potatoes?

8) What city was the first U.S. national capital?

9) Who was the first elected head of a nation to give birth in office?

10) During WWII when Hitler visited Paris, what did the French do to the Eiffel Tower?

Quiz 28 Answers

1) Albert Einstein

2) Weather forecast

3) Blackbeard the pirate

4) Owl – She carried it in her pocket.

5) Herodotus

6) Olive oil – They rubbed it into their skin and then scraped it off along with dirt and dead skin.

7) Belgium - late 17th century

8) Philadelphia, Pennsylvania

9) Benazir Bhutto – Pakistan in 1990

10) They cut the lift cables, so Hitler would have to climb the steps if he wanted to go to the top.

Quiz 29

1) What was Gandhi's profession?

2) In what country did coffee originate?

3) What nationality was Cleopatra?

4) How tall was Napoleon?

5) What date was V.E. Day?

6) What British prime minister's mother was born in Brooklyn, New York?

7) What two mountain ranges did Hannibal and his elephants march through in 218 BC?

8) What was the D–Day invasion password?

9) Which side did Britain support in the U.S. Civil War?

10) What year followed 1 BC?

Quiz 29 Answers

1) Lawyer

2) Ethiopia – 11th century

3) Greek

4) 5 feet 7 inches - The average adult French male of his time was 5 feet 5 inches, so he was taller than average; some of the confusion is the units his height was reported in and that his personal guards who he was usually seen with were required to be quite tall.

5) May 8, 1945

6) Winston Churchill

7) Pyrenees and Alps

8) Mickey Mouse

9) Confederacy

10) 1 AD

Quiz 30

1) What pope died 33 days after his election?

2) What country contains the Waterloo battlefield?

3) The rallying cry "Remember the Maine!" came from what war?

4) What was Al Capone finally imprisoned for in 1931?

5) Who reached the South Pole in January 1912 only to find that Amundsen had gotten there first?

6) What cities were the two original end points of the Orient Express' run?
7) What ancient marvel did Nebuchadnezzar build?
8) Who invented the automobile in 1885?
9) What war did Florence Nightingale tend troops in?
10) What amendment to the U.S. Constitution ended prohibition?

Quiz 30 Answers

1) John Paul I
2) Belgium
3) Spanish–American War
4) Income tax evasion
5) Captain Robert Scott
6) Istanbul and Paris
7) Hanging Gardens of Babylon
8) Karl Benz
9) Crimean
10) 21st

Quiz 31

1) How many stars were on the U.S flag in 1913?
2) Who founded the De Beers mining company?
3) Who was the first president of independent Texas?
4) Where did two jumbo jets collide in 1977, killing 579?
5) **What were the original seven wonders of the ancient world?**
6) What fighting unit is headquartered in Corsica?
7) What war caused the most American deaths?
8) What was the first railroad to cross the U.S.?
9) Who was the first American in space?
10) Who was Helen Keller's teacher?

Quiz 31 Answers

1) 48 – Alaska and Hawaii weren't states yet.

2) Cecil Rhodes

3) Sam Houston

4) Tenerife, Canary Islands

5) **Great Pyramid of Giza, Colossus of Rhodes, Lighthouse of Alexandria, Mausoleum at Halicarnassus, Temple of Artemis at Ephesus, Statue of Zeus at Olympia, Hanging Gardens of Babylon**

6) French Foreign Legion

7) Civil War

8) Union Pacific

9) Alan Shepard Jr.

10) Anne Sullivan

Quiz 32

1) What two European countries entered the American Revolutionary War on the side of the Americans?

2) Who was the defense lawyer in the Scopes Monkey Trial?

3) Who was the second man on the Moon?

4) What country declared war on both Germany and the Allies in WWII?

5) What famous heist did Ronald Biggs mastermind?

6) What is the claim to fame of Chang and Eng Bunker?

7) What caused 20 million deaths in 1918?

8) Who was the Iron Chancellor of Germany?

9) What was American folk hero John Chapman's nickname?

10) What date was Hiroshima bombed?

Quiz 32 Answers

1) France and Spain

2) Clarence Darrow

3) Buzz Aldrin

4) Italy – One month after surrendering to the allies, Italy declared war on Germany, its former ally.

5) Great Train Robbery

6) Original Siamese twins

7) Influenza
8) Otto von Bismarck
9) Johnny Appleseed
10) August 6, 1945

Quiz 33

1) Who is the longest reigning British monarch?
2) How did Socrates commit suicide?
3) Who inherited the throne of Scotland at the age of six days?
4) Who headed the Gestapo?
5) What two countries did Hadrian's wall separate?
6) What was the first country to legalize abortion in 1935?
7) Who did Winston Churchill succeed as British prime minister at the outbreak of WWII?
8) What was the third country to develop an atomic bomb?
9) How many people were executed for Abraham Lincoln's assassination?
10) Who taught the theory of evolution in 1925 contrary to Tennessee law?

Quiz 33 Answers

1) Queen Elizabeth II – She surpassed her great-great-grandmother Victoria's reign in 2015.
2) Drank poison hemlock
3) Mary, Queen of Scots or Mary I
4) Heinrich Himmler
5) England and Scotland
6) Iceland
7) Neville Chamberlain
8) Great Britain
9) Four
10) John T. Scopes – Scopes Monkey Trial

Quiz 34

1) How many manned *Apollo* flights preceded the Moon landing?
2) What Spanish soldier of fortune led the expedition that discovered the Pacific Ocean?
3) What country did the Romans call Hibernia?
4) What was the name of Charles Darwin's survey ship?
5) What car brand was named for the founder of Detroit, Michigan?
6) What river is Pocahontas buried along?
7) What was the name of the B-29 that dropped the bomb on Hiroshima?
8) Who was the most decorated U.S. soldier of WWII?
9) Who was America's first public enemy number one?
10) What ship collided with the Swedish liner *Stockholm* on July 26, 1956?

Quiz 34 Answers

1) Four
2) Vasco Balboa
3) Ireland
4) Beagle
5) Cadillac – French explorer Antoine de la Mothe Cadillac founded Detroit in 1701.
6) Thames in England
7) *Enola Gay*
8) Audie Murphy
9) John Dillinger
10) *Andrea Doria*

Quiz 35

1) Who was accused in The Trial of the Century which opened January 1, 1935?
2) What are the five permanent members of the United Nations Security Council?
3) Sunglasses were invented in China to do what?

4) Who was the first U.S. Postmaster General?

5) The only woman ever awarded the U.S. Medal of Honor received it for her service in what war?

6) What New York Fifth Avenue store supplied the Union army with swords and surgical instruments during the Civil War?

7) How many years did the U.S. Congress allow for voluntary conversion to the metric system in legislation passed in 1975?

8) Who was the first person to circumnavigate Antarctica?

9) What country was the first to allow women to vote in 1893?

10) Who is the youngest American astronaut to travel in space?

Quiz 35 Answers

1) Bruno Richard Hauptmann – Lindbergh kidnapping

2) United States, United Kingdom, France, Russia, China

3) Hide the eyes of judges

4) Benjamin Franklin

5) Civil War – Mary Edwards Walker was a surgeon at a temporary Washington, D.C. hospital and was captured and arrested as a spy after crossing enemy lines to treat wounded civilians.

6) Tiffany's

7) 10

8) James Cook – 1773

9) New Zealand

10) Sally Ride - 32

Literature

Quiz 1

1) Who wrote *Oedipus Rex*?
2) What is the only Shakespeare play that mentions America?
3) In the original book *The Wonderful Wizard of Oz*, what color are the slippers?
4) Where did Winnie the Pooh live?
5) Who wrote *Wuthering Heights*?
6) What writer coined the term "atomic bomb" approximately 30 years before its invention?
7) By what name is the fictional character Duchess of Saint Bridget better known as?
8) Who wrote *Dracula*?
9) In *Treasure Island*, what was Long John Silver's job when on board ship?
10) Where did Clark Kent attend college?

Quiz 1 Answers

1) Sophocles
2) *The Comedy of Errors*
3) Silver
4) Hundred Acre Wood
5) Emily Bronte
6) H.G. Wells
7) Lara Croft
8) Bram Stoker
9) Quartermaster – handles the ship's food and drink
10) Metropolis University

Quiz 2

1) What Stephen King novel features a villain who sometimes goes by the alias Bob Gray?

2) What does the J.K. stand for in Harry Potter author J.K. Rowling's name?

3) Edward Nigma is the birth name of what Batman foe?

4) Who wrote *Breakfast at Tiffany's*?

5) How many lines does a sonnet have?

6) In *Charlotte's Web*, what is the name of the gluttonous rat?

7) What Shakespeare play features the line "All the world's a stage, and all the men and women merely players"?

8) What well known Russian author was also a doctor?

9) What are the two family names central to Shakespeare's *Romeo and Juliet*?

10) What poet won the Pulitzer Prize four times?

Quiz 2 Answers

1) *It*
2) Joanne Kathleen
3) Riddler
4) Truman Capote
5) 14
6) Templeton
7) *As You Like It*
8) Anton Chekov
9) Capulets and Montagues
10) Robert Frost

Quiz 3

1) In Rudyard Kipling's poem "Gunga Din", what is Gunga Din's role for the British army?

2) In *The Canterbury Tales*, what were the pilgrims traveling to visit?

3) Who wrote *Doctor Zhivago*?

4) What was the first fictional novel blessed by the pope?

5) Which Shakespeare play is set in the Forest of Arden?

6) Edgar Allan Poe created mystery fiction's first detective in what 1841 story?

7) Who wrote *The Hitchhikers Guide to the Galaxy*?

8) In *Little Women*, what is the sisters surname?

9) What Shakespeare play has the line "Now is the winter of our discontent"?

10) What Is the name of the evil slave owner and villain in *Uncle Tom's Cabin*?

Quiz 3 Answers

1) Water bearer
2) Thomas Becket's tomb
3) Boris Pasternak
4) *Ben-Hur: A Tale of the Christ*
5) *As You Like It*
6) *The Murders in the Rue Morgue*
7) Douglas Adams
8) March
9) *Richard III*
10) Simon Legree

Quiz 4

1) What does the J.R.R. stand for in J.R.R. Tolkien?
2) Who wrote the book on which the film *Jurassic Park* is based?
3) Who wrote *The Strange Case of Dr. Jekyll and Mr. Hyde*?
4) In *Gulliver's Travels*, what is Gulliver's profession?
5) What was Shakespeare's last completed play?
6) Who is the author of *All Creatures Great and Small*?
7) In comics, who is the alter ego of Selina Kyle?
8) What is the title of Charles Dickens' unfinished novel?
9) Who wrote *The Chronicles of Narnia*?
10) Who published *Poor Richard's Almanack*?

Quiz 4 Answers

1) John Ronald Reuel
2) Michael Crichton

3) Robert Louis Stevenson

4) Surgeon

5) *The Tempest*

6) James Herriot

7) Catwoman

8) *The Mystery of Edwin Drood*

9) C.S. Lewis

10) Benjamin Franklin

Quiz 5

1) What award is the mystery writer's equivalent of an Oscar?

2) Who wrote *Valley of the Dolls*?

3) What Ray Bradbury novel is named for the temperature at which paper catches fire?

4) Pip is the hero in what Charles Dickens novel?

5) Edmond Dantes is better known as what literary hero?

6) What novelist sometimes writes under the pseudonym Richard Bachman?

7) Who was born at Daisy Hill Puppy Farm?

8) What author has the most entries on the *New York Times* best-seller list?

9) Who killed Macbeth?

10) What international best-selling author also wrote under the name Mary Westmacott?

Quiz 5 Answers

1) Edgar – after Edgar Allan Poe

2) Jacqueline Susann

3) *Fahrenheit 451*

4) *Great Expectations*

5) Count of Monte Cristo

6) Stephen King

7) Snoopy

8) James Patterson

9) Macduff

10) Agatha Christie

Quiz 6

1) What Shakespeare character's last words are "Thus with a kiss I die"?

2) What 18th century writer first penned the line "For fools rush in where angels fear to tread"?

3) Barbara Gordon is better known as what comic book alter ego?

4) *There and Back Again* is an alternative title of what novel?

5) Who wrote a series of novels about CIA analyst Jack Ryan?

6) What author's thrillers include *The Osterman Weekend* and *The Prometheus Deception*?

7) Who wrote *The Rime of the Ancient Mariner*?

8) What private eye hero did Raymond Chandler create?

9) Who told stories about Brer Rabbit and Brer Fox?

10) What is the surname of the family in *The Grapes of Wrath*?

Quiz 6 Answers

1) Romeo

2) Alexander Pope

3) Batgirl

4) *The Hobbit*

5) Tom Clancy

6) Robert Ludlum

7) Samuel Taylor Coleridge

8) Philip Marlowe

9) Uncle Remus

10) Joad

Quiz 7

1) Who was the first man to appear on the cover of *Playboy*?

2) Who in literature is told to "Begin at the beginning and go on till you come to the end; then stop"?

3) Who wrote *The Call of the Wild*?

4) Who created Perry Mason?

5) In Sherlock Holmes, what is Professor Moriarty's first name?

6) What country originated the story of Cinderella?

7) What Dr. Seuss tale is set "on the 15th of May, in the jungle of Nool, in the heat of the day, in the cool of the pool"?

8) What famous character did Jean de Brunhoff create in 1931?

9) What was Shakespeare's first play?

10) Who wrote the play *Androcles and the Lion*?

Quiz 7 Answers

1) Peter Sellers

2) Alice – *Alice's Adventures in Wonderland*

3) Jack London

4) Erle Stanley Gardner

5) James

6) China

7) *Horton Hears a Who!*

8) Babar the Elephant

9) *Henry VI*

10) George Bernard Shaw

Quiz 8

1) What Shakespeare play ends in marriage of Benedick and Beatrice?

2) Who wrote *Interview with a Vampire*?

3) *My Fair Lady* is based on what George Bernard Shaw play?

4) Who wrote *Charlie and the Chocolate Factory*?

5) What book contains the line "It is a truth universally acknowledged that a single man in possession of a good fortune must be in want of a wife"?

6) In Shakespeare's *The Taming of the Shrew*, what is the name of the shrew?

7) Who wrote the Father Brown crime stories?

8) What is the title of William Golding's book about boys marooned on

an island?

9) Who first wrote about the lost civilization of Atlantis?

10) What is the name of Gandalf's horse?

Quiz 8 Answers

1) *Much Ado About Nothing*

2) Ann Rice

3) *Pygmalion*

4) Roald Dahl

5) *Pride and Prejudice*

6) Katherine or Kate

7) G.K. Chesterton

8) *Lord of the Flies*

9) Plato

10) Shadowfax

Quiz 9

1) What did Dr. Seuss write after his editor dared him to write a book using fewer than 50 different words?

2) Michael Bond created what children's character?

3) Who was Dr. Zhivago's great love?

4) Miss Felicity Lemon is what fictional detective's confidential secretary?

5) In the Grimm's fairy tale, the *Pied Piper of Hamelin* is described as pied because he does what?

6) The Newbery Medal is given annually for what?

7) Both Katharine Ross and Nicole Kidman have played Joanna Eberhart, the main character from what novel?

8) What London club does Mycroft Holmes belong to?

9) What book begins with the line "When he was nearly thirteen, my brother Jem got his arm badly broken at the elbow"?

10) Who wrote *The Count of Monte Cristo*?

Quiz 9 Answers

1) *Green Eggs and Ham*
2) Paddington Bear
3) Lara
4) Hercule Poirot
5) Wears a two-colored coat – Pied is thought to come from magpies which are black and white.
6) Best children's book
7) *The Stepford Wives*
8) Diogenes
9) *To Kill a Mockingbird*
10) Alexandre Dumas

Quiz 10

1) According to Ernest Hemmingway, there are only three sports; what are they?
2) Who wrote *Crime and Punishment*?
3) What is the best-selling fiction book of all time?
4) Who wrote *2001: A Space Odyssey*?
5) Who is the most widely translated author in the world?
6) What was the title of Niccolo Machiavelli's book published in 1532?
7) Who does Sherlock Holmes refer to as "The Woman"?
8) Who wrote *To Kill a Mockingbird*?
9) What is the secret identity of Don Diego de la Vega?
10) What writer established the three laws of robotics?

Quiz 10 Answers

1) Bullfighting, motor racing, mountaineering – According to Hemingway, "All the rest are merely games."
2) Fyodor Dostoevsky
3) *Don Quixote* – estimated 500 million copies
4) Arthur C. Clarke
5) Agatha Christie

6) *The Prince*

7) Irene Adler

8) Harper Lee

9) Zorro

10) Isaac Asimov

Quiz 11

1) What is Tarzan's real identity?

2) What crime novelist created the character Mike Hammer?

3) What classic novel is based on the adventures of Alexander Selkirk, an early 18th-century Scottish sailor?

4) P.L. Travers created what famous character?

5) Who took dictation from Perry Mason?

6) What novel has the line "Four legs good, two legs bad"?

7) Who wrote *The Caine Mutiny*?

8) Who is Oscar Zoroaster Phadrig Isaac Norman Henkle Immanuel Ambrose Diggs?

9) Who ate Chicken Little?

10) Who first wrote, "Do not count your chickens before they are hatched"?

Quiz 11 Answers

1) Lord Greystoke

2) Mickey Spillane

3) *Robinson Crusoe*

4) Mary Poppins

5) Della Street

6) *Animal Farm*

7) Herman Wouk

8) The Wizard of Oz

9) Foxy Loxy or Foxy Woxy

10) Aesop – *The Milkmaid and Her Pail*

Quiz 12

1) What children's classic did Johann David Wyss write?
2) What children's book features the adventures of a boy named Milo and a watchdog named Tock?
3) In comics, Linda Lee Danvers is whose alter ego?
4) Who is the alter ego of the Incredible Hulk?
5) What was the first story to feature Sherlock Holmes?
6) British mathematician Charles Lutwidge Dodgson is better known by what pen name?
7) Who declined the 1964 Nobel Prize for literature?
8) According to Ernest Hemmingway, a man must plant a tree, fight a bull, have a son, and what other thing to be man?
9) What book won the very first Nebula Award for best science fiction or fantasy novel in 1966?
10) Who was the first *Playboy* centerfold?

Quiz 12 Answers

1) *The Swiss Family Robinson*
2) *The Phantom Tollbooth*
3) Supergirl
4) Dr. David Banner
5) *A Study in Scarlet*
6) Lewis Carroll – *Alice's Adventures in Wonderland*
7) Jean-Paul Sartre
8) Write a book
9) *Dune*
10) Marilyn Monroe

Quiz 13

1) What year was the first issue of *National Geographic* published?
2) What was the first U.S. digital media company to win a Pulitzer Prize?
3) Who was the first woman to win both a Pulitzer Prize and Nobel Prize for literature?

4) The Artful Dodger is a character from what novel?

5) What was Tom Clancy's first novel?

6) Who was the first American to win the Nobel Prize for literature?

7) How many books are in *The Chronicles of Narnia* series by C.S. Lewis?

8) Who is the Green Hornet's alter ego?

9) Civil War Union general Lewis Wallace wrote what book that later became a famous movie?

10) Who wrote the *Game of Thrones* book series?

Quiz 13 Answers

1) 1888

2) *The Huffington Post*

3) Pearl S. Buck

4) *Oliver Twist*

5) *The Hunt for Red October*

6) Sinclair Lewis – 1930

7) Seven

8) Britt Reed

9) *Ben-Hur: A Tale of the Christ*

10) George R.R. Martin

Quiz 14

1) Who wrote *The Little Mermaid*?

2) Whose image is engraved on the Pulitzer Prize gold medals?

3) Psychologist William Marston was one of the inventors of the polygraph, and he also created what well known comics character?

4) What poem by John Milton tells the story of Adam and Eve's temptation and the fall of man?

5) What is Scarlett O'Hara's real first name in *Gone with the Wind*?

6) In *The Jungle Book*, what is the name of the boy?

7) Who was Truman Capote's best friend and next-door neighbor that he first met when he was five years old?

8) What was the first daily comic strip to win a Pulitzer Prize for best editorial cartoon?

9) What is the best-selling science fiction book of all time?

10) According to the *Guinness Book of World Records*, what single author has the most published works?

Quiz 14 Answers

1) Hans Christian Andersen

2) Benjamin Franklin

3) Wonder Woman

4) *Paradise Lost* – 1667

5) Katie – Scarlett is her middle name.

6) Mowgli

7) Harper Lee – author of *To Kill a Mockingbird*

8) *Doonesbury*

9) *Dune*

10) L. Ron Hubbard – 1,084

Quiz 15

1) What news organization has won the most Pulitzer Prizes?

2) Who coined the word tween?

3) What is Shakespeare's longest play?

4) What is Wonder Woman's alter ego?

5) *The Communist Manifesto* was written by what two German philosophers?

6) Who wrote the poem "The Song of Hiawatha"?

7) What was the best-selling American fiction book of the 19th century?

8) Writer Eric Blair went by what pen name?

9) What institution awards the Pulitzer Prizes?

10) Who was the first English language writer to win the Nobel Prize for literature?

Quiz 15 Answers

1) New York Times

2) J.R.R. Tolkien – In *The Hobbit*, it is used to describe Hobbits in their

reckless age period.

3) Hamlet
4) Diana Prince
5) Karl Marx and Friedrich Engels
6) Henry Wadsworth Longfellow
7) *Uncle Tom's Cabin*
8) George Orwell
9) Columbia University
10) Rudyard Kipling

Quiz 16

1) How old is Juliet in Shakespeare's *Romeo and Juliet*?
2) Who edited Michael Jackson's autobiography *Moonwalk*?
3) Who wrote *Don Quixote*?
4) Crab, the only named dog in any Shakespeare play, appears in what play?
5) Who wrote *Robinson Crusoe*?
6) What was Dr. Frankenstein's first name?
7) What American novel was the first to sell 1 million copies?
8) What is the name of the gypsy girl Quasimodo falls in love with in *The Hunchback of Notre Dame*?
9) Who wrote *Catch-22*?
10) What book opens with the line "It was the best of times, it was the worst of times"?

Quiz 16 Answers

1) 13
2) Jacqueline Kennedy Onassis
3) Miguel de Cervantes
4) *Two Gentlemen of Verona*
5) Daniel Defoe
6) Victor
7) *Uncle Tom's Cabin*
8) Esmeralda

9) Joseph Heller

10) *A Tale of Two Cities*

Quiz 17

1) What comics character has the maiden name Boopadoop?
2) What book is subtitled *The Boy Who Wouldn't Grow Up*?
3) Who wrote *The Secret Life of Walter Mitty*?
4) What novel is set in a desert with giant sandworms?
5) Who is the only author to publish books in nine of the ten Dewey Decimal categories?
6) What is the last line of Dickens's *A Christmas Carol*?
7) What novel has the subtitle *The Modern Prometheus*?
8) Who wrote the play *Our Town*?
9) What is the name of the pig in *Charlotte's Web*?
10) Who wrote *Black Beauty*?

Quiz 17 Answers

1) Blondie Bumstead
2) *Peter Pan*
3) James Thurber
4) *Dune*
5) Isaac Asimov
6) God bless us, everyone!
7) *Frankenstein*
8) Thornton Wilder
9) Wilbur
10) Anna Sewell

Quiz 18

1) Who wrote the poem "Paul Revere's Ride"?
2) Who wrote, "If god did not exist, it would be necessary to invent him"?
3) What was Charles Dickens first novel?
4) Who wrote, "How do I love thee? Let me count the ways"?

5) *Just One More Thing* is an autobiography by what actor?

6) What does DC stand for in DC Comics?

7) Holden Caulfield appears in what novel?

8) What is the first name of Gatsby in *The Great Gatsby*?

9) What is Shakespeare's shortest play?

10) Lenny Small and George Milton are the main characters in what novel?

Quiz 18 Answers

1) Henry Wadsworth Longfellow

2) Voltaire – 1770

3) *The Pickwick Papers*

4) Elizabeth Barrett Browning

5) Peter Falk

6) Detective Comics

7) *Catcher in the Rye*

8) Jay

9) *The Comedy of Errors*

10) *Of Mice and Men*

Quiz 19

1) What fictional doctor is the main character in a series of books by Hugh Lofting?

2) Fictional character Sir Percy Blakeney is better known as who?

3) Oliver Mellors is the lover of what fictional character?

4) Who wrote *The Wonderful Wizard of Oz*?

5) Who wrote the *Twilight* series of books?

6) What was the name of Don Quixote's love?

7) In *The Jungle Book*, what is the name of the bear?

8) What are the names of Peter Cottontail's sisters in *The Tale of Peter Rabbit*?

9) What author was the first to use the word nerd in print?

10) What was the first James Bond book?

Quiz 19 Answers

1) Doctor Dolittle
2) The Scarlet Pimpernel
3) Lady Chatterley
4) L. Frank Baum
5) Stephenie Meyer
6) Dulcinea
7) Baloo
8) Flopsy, Mopsy, Cottontail
9) Dr. Seuss – name of a creature in *If I Ran the Zoo* in 1950
10) *Casino Royale*

Quiz 20

1) Who wrote *The Man in the Iron Mask*?
2) Whose autobiography was *The Long Walk to Freedom*?
3) Who wrote *Pride and Prejudice*?
4) Who wrote *Gulliver's Travels*?
5) The title of whose book translates as *My Struggle*?
6) Carlo Collodi created what children's character?
7) In what book are there Eloi and Morlocks?
8) In what book would you find the servant Passepartout?
9) Who created Tarzan?
10) What literary character was the Thane of Cawdor?

Quiz 20 Answers

1) Alexandre Dumas
2) Nelson Mandela
3) Jane Austen
4) Jonathan Swift
5) Adolf Hitler – *Mein Kampf*
6) Pinocchio
7) *The Time Machine*

8) *Around the World in 80 Days*

9) Edgar Rice Burroughs

10) Macbeth

Quiz 21

1) Who created the characters Sam Spade and Nick and Nora Charles?

2) In *Moby Dick*, what is the name of Captain Ahab's ship?

3) What was writer O. Henry's real name?

4) Ernest Hemmingway's *The Old Man and the Sea* is set in what country?

5) What author has the most films based on their work?

6) Who is generally credited with first saying, "When in doubt tell the truth"?

7) Who wrote *Little Men*?

8) What was Stephen King's first published novel?

9) What links *The Reivers*, *The Grapes of Wrath*, and *Humboldt's Gift*?

10) Who wrote *The Picture of Dorian Gray*?

Quiz 21 Answers

1) Dashiell Hammett

2) Pequod

3) William Sydney Porter

4) Cuba

5) William Shakespeare

6) Mark Twain

7) Louisa May Alcott

8) *Carrie*

9) Pulitzer Prize fiction winners

10) Oscar Wilde

Quiz 22

1) What author created the character The Saint?

2) When Lord Byron became a student at Cambridge, dogs were prohibited; what did he get as a pet?

3) Who wrote *The Wind in the Willows*?

4) Who wrote *Charlotte's Web*?

5) What novelist is known as the father of science fiction?

6) Who is the only person to have their own Dewey Decimal classification?

7) Who wrote *Jane Eyre*?

8) Who wrote *The Scarlet Letter*?

9) In *A Christmas Carol*, what is the name of the employer that Scrooge works for in his youth?

10) The Caldecott Medal is given for what?

Quiz 22 Answers

1) Leslie Charteris

2) A bear – The bear stayed in his lodgings, and Byron would take him for walks around the grounds.

3) **Kenneth Grahame**

4) E.B. White

5) Jules Verne

6) William Shakespeare

7) **Charlotte Bronte**

8) Nathaniel Hawthorne

9) Fezziwig

10) Children's book illustration

Quiz 23

1) What playwright choked to death on the cap of a bottle of barbiturates?

2) What famous Spanish and English writers died on the same day – April 23, 1616?

3) **Who wrote *The Red Badge of Courage*?**

4) Who is Bertie Wooster's butler?

5) Who wrote *Uncle Tom's Cabin*?

6) **What Missouri town was Mark Twain's boyhood home?**

7) What mountains did Rip Van Winkle nod off in?

8) Who wrote *In Cold Blood*?
9) Who wrote the poem "The Road Not Taken"?
10) What play recounts the last hours of Willy Loman?

Quiz 23 Answers

1) Tennessee Williams
2) Miguel de Cervantes and William Shakespeare
3) **Stephen Crane**
4) Jeeves – from the novels of P.G. Wodehouse
5) Harriet Beecher Stowe
6) **Hannibal**
7) Catskills
8) **Truman Capote**
9) Robert Frost
10) *Death of a Salesman*

Quiz 24

1) What is the last name of Lucy and Linus from the Peanuts cartoon?
2) Who said, "The end justifies the means"?
3) What Shakespeare play features Rosencrantz and Guildenstern?
4) What is Richard Bach's best-selling adult fairy tale?
5) Who wrote, "Poems are made by fools like me, but only god can make a tree"?
6) Who was the first novelist to present a typed manuscript to their publisher?
7) Who created Winnie the Pooh?
8) What Pulitzer Prize winning play dramatized the life of African American boxing champ Jack Johnson?
9) Who created British master spy George Smiley?
10) What Richard Adams book includes an account of Bigwig's encounter with a fox?

Quiz 24 Answers

1) Van Pelt

2) Niccolò Machiavelli
3) *Hamlet*
4) *Jonathon Livingston Seagull*
5) Joyce Kilmer
6) Mark Twain
7) A.A. Milne
8) *The Great White Hope*
9) John le Carre
10) *Watership Down*

Quiz 25

1) Who wrote *Of Mice and Men*?
2) Who wrote *The Exorcist*?
3) In comics, who is the editor of *The Daily Planet*?
4) What epic chronicles events toward the end of the Trojan wars?
5) What James Dickey novel tells the tale of an ill-fated canoe trip?
6) What was the name of the fisherman in Hemingway's *The Old Man and the Sea*?
7) Who wrote *East of Eden*?
8) How many ghosts appear to Scrooge in Dickens' *A Christmas Carol*?
9) As originally written, what nationality was Aladdin?
10) What American poet wrote a four-volume biography of Abraham Lincoln?

Quiz 25 Answers

1) John Steinbeck
2) William Peter Blatty
3) Perry White
4) *The Iliad*
5) *Deliverance*
6) Santiago
7) John Steinbeck
8) Four – Marley, past, present, and yet to come

9) Chinese
10) Carl Sandburg

Quiz 26

1) What American poet wrote, "Good fences make good neighbors"?
2) Who was Don Quixote's sidekick?
3) Who created Peter Rabbit?
4) **Who wrote *The Black Stallion*?**
5) What nursery rhyme character had arachnophobia?
6) What phenomenon appeared the day Mark Twain was born and the day he died?
7) Who created Billy Pilgrim, a survivor of the Dresden firestorm?
8) What novel features the character First Lieutenant Milo Minderbinder?
9) Who wrote *The Razor's Edge*?
10) What Shakespeare play contains the line "Something is rotten in the state of Denmark"?

Quiz 26 Answers

1) Robert Frost
2) Sancho Panza
3) Beatrix Potter
4) **Walter Farley**
5) Little Miss Muffet
6) Halley's Comet
7) Kurt Vonnegut Jr. – *Slaughterhouse-Five*
8) *Catch-22*
9) Somerset Maugham
10) *Hamlet*

Quiz 27

1) What poet wrote, "I have promises to keep, and miles to go before I sleep"?
2) What fictional detective retired to become a beekeeper?

3) What is the nationality of Agatha Christie's detective Hercule Poirot?

4) What imaginary island did Sir Thomas More created in a 1516 work?

5) How many known plays did William Shakespeare write?

6) What was H.G. Wells' first novel?

7) Who wrote, "A thing of beauty is a joy for ever"?

8) What were the names of the three Bronte sisters?

9) What book opens with, "Somewhere in la Mancha, in a place whose name I do not care to remember"?

10) Who wrote *The Glass Menagerie*?

Quiz 27 Answers

1) Robert Frost

2) Sherlock Holmes

3) Belgian

4) Utopia

5) 37

6) *The Time Machine*

7) John Keats

8) Anne, Charlotte, Emily

9) *Don Quixote*

10) Tennessee Williams

Quiz 28

1) Who wrote *The Prince and the Pauper*?

2) Who wrote about the lioness Elsa in *Born Free*, *Living Free*, and *Forever Free*?

3) Who wrote *The Guns of Navarone*?

4) In what Shakespeare play does the character Caliban appear?

5) In what book did the utopia Shangri-La appear?

6) Who wrote the *Jungle Book* series?

7) What Stephen King story is set at Cold Mountain Penitentiary?

8) Who titled the first of her 723 novels *Jigsaw* in 1925?

9) Who wrote *Ivanhoe*?

10) Who created the fictional detective Nero Wolfe?

Quiz 28 Answers

1)   Mark Twain
2)   Joy Adamson
3)   Alistair MacLean
4)   *The Tempest*
5)   *Lost Horizon*
6)   Rudyard Kipling
7)   *The Green Mile*
8)   Barbara Cartland
9)   Sir Walter Scott
10) Rex Stout

Quiz 29

1)   Who wrote *Tom Jones*?
2)   What are the tree like creatures in *The Lord of the Rings* called?
3)   Who wrote *The Importance of Being Ernest*?
4)   What is Winnie the Pooh's real name?
5)   In Shakespeare's *The Taming of the Shrew*, who tamed the shrew?
6)   Who wrote *Lady Chatterley's Lover*?
7)   Who is the only person to win four Pulitzer Prizes for drama?
8)   Who wrote *Pilgrim's Progress*?
9)   Who is the only African American woman to win the Nobel Prize for literature?
10) Who wrote *A Passage to India*?

Quiz 29 Answers

1)   Henry Fielding
2)   Ents
3)   Oscar Wilde
4)   Edward Bear
5)   Petruchio

6) D.H. Lawrence
7) Eugene O'Neill
8) John Bunyan
9) Toni Morrison
10) E.M. Forster

Miscellaneous

Quiz 1

1) How did the term "piggy bank" originate?
2) What does the word karaoke literally mean?
3) What is enuresis?
4) What is a digamy?
5) In 1892, Juan Vucetich was the first person to solve a crime using what?
6) Who was the first pilot to fly faster than the speed of sound?
7) The hard piece at the end of a shoelace is called what?
8) What is the only number spelled out in English that has the same number of letters as its value?
9) The U.S. $10,000 bill was last printed in 1945 and is the largest denomination ever in public circulation; whose portrait appeared on it?
10) What is the original name for the pound or number symbol (#)?

Quiz 1 Answers

1) Pygg clay – An orange clay called pygg was used to make dishes and jars that were sometimes used to hold spare change. At some point, people decided to use pygg clay to make pig-shaped banks.
2) Empty orchestra
3) Bedwetting
4) A second legal marriage after death or divorce
5) Fingerprints
6) Chuck Yeager
7) Aglet
8) Four
9) Salmon P. Chase – Secretary of the Treasury
10) Octothorpe – It is believed to have been made up by workers at Bell Telephone Labs who needed a name for the symbol on the telephone keypad.

Quiz 2

1) What country consumes the most coffee per capita?
2) According to the Bible, how long did Methuselah live?
3) What is the name of the dog on the Cracker Jack box?
4) What vegetable did Mark Twain describe as "cabbage with a college education"?
5) What country eats the most chocolate per capita?
6) If you have a buccula, what have you got?
7) What is the longest railway line in the world?
8) In what country were fortune cookies invented?
9) What country has the highest per capita consumption of turkey?
10) Who was the first person other than royalty to appear on a British stamp?

Quiz 2 Answers

1) Finland
2) 969 years
3) Bingo
4) Cauliflower
5) Switzerland
6) Double chin
7) Trans–Siberian Railway – 5,772 miles
8) United States
9) Israel
10) William Shakespeare

Quiz 3

1) What is the only number spelled out in English that has letters in alphabetical order?
2) What are camel hair brushes typically made from?
3) What game has the most books written about it?
4) The feeling from hitting your funny bone is due to hitting what?
5) What is the most popular crop in U.S. home gardens?

6) Frank Lloyd Wright's son John invented what after watching workers move timber?

7) What kind of condition is protanopia?

8) What was Queen Victoria prescribed for her menstrual cramps?

9) What was the first type of product sold in aerosol spray cans?

10) Before 1938, toothbrushes were made using hairs from what?

Quiz 3 Answers

1) Forty
2) Squirrel hair
3) Chess
4) Ulnar nerve
5) Tomatoes
6) Lincoln Logs
7) Color blindness
8) Marijuana
9) Insecticide
10) Boar

Quiz 4

1) What well known economist studied clarinet performance at Juilliard?

2) What familiar word is derived from a Latin word that means "place where three roads meet"?

3) Acmegenesis is better known as what?

4) What globally successful product was created by Dr. John Pemberton?

5) Who was eaten by dogs in the Bible?

6) What was the name of the apostle who replaced Judas Iscariot?

7) Gail Borden invented what food item?

8) Since pigs don't sweat much, where does the expression "sweat like a pig" come from?

9) What is the study of bumps on the head called?

10) What color is an aircraft's black box flight recorder?

Quiz 4 Answers

1) Alan Greenspan
2) Trivia
3) Orgasm
4) Coca-Cola
5) Jezebel
6) Matthias
7) Condensed milk
8) It comes from the iron smelting process. Iron ore was smelted into pig iron which got its name because the mold the iron was poured into had ingots at right angles to a center channel and resembled a litter of piglets suckling on their mother. They knew the pig iron was cool enough to transport when it started to sweat from condensation as it cooled which originated the term "sweat like a pig".
9) Phrenology
10) Orange

Quiz 5

1) A cluster of 10-20 bananas is called what?
2) Cognac must be at least five years old before it's labeled what?
3) What does a month beginning on a Sunday always have?
4) What carbonated beverage started out in the 1890s as Brad's Drink?
5) What was the first nationally distributed beer in the U.S.?
6) A standard barrel of crude oil holds roughly how many gallons?
7) Who was the first member of the British royal family to graduate from a university?
8) In what country did chocolate originate?
9) The term "slush fund" was originally used by sailors to refer to the side money they made selling what?
10) Orienteering began in what country?

Quiz 5 Answers

1) A hand

2) Napoleon
3) Friday the 13th
4) Pepsi
5) Budweiser
6) 42
7) Prince Charles
8) Mexico
9) Animal fat – Sailors sold the fat or grease from the meat cooked on board to tallow makers.
10) Sweden

Quiz 6

1) According to the Bible, how tall is Goliath?
2) What was the first product to have a barcode?
3) The dot over the letter "i" is called what?
4) "Fidelity, Bravery, and Integrity" is which U.S. organization's motto?
5) A gross is equal to 144 units; how many units are in a great gross?
6) What toy was originally called the Pluto Platter?
7) What country invented cheesecake?
8) In terms of production volume, what is the most popular fruit in the world?
9) What country has the highest per capita tea consumption?
10) What merchandise brand was created by Adolf Dassler?

Quiz 6 Answers

1) Six cubits - about nine feet
2) Wrigley's gum
3) Tittle
4) FBI
5) 1728 – 12 gross
6) Frisbee
7) Greece
8) Tomato – The tomato is technically a fruit.

9) Turkey

10) Adidas

Quiz 7

1) The largest named wine bottle size is Melchizedek; how large is it?
2) Who is the largest toy distributor in the world?
3) What are the ridges on corduroy called?
4) What year did the first canned beer go on sale in the U.S.?
5) Who or what are taikonauts?
6) What is the cultivation of grapes known as?
7) What is the world's best-selling candy bar?
8) The practice of performing in public places for tips and gratuities is known as what?
9) What country consumes the most Coca-Cola per capita?
10) What causes a jumping bean to jump?

Quiz 7 Answers

1) 30 liters – equivalent to 40 standard 750 ml wine bottles
2) McDonald's – About 20% of its meals are Happy Meals with a toy.
3) Wales
4) 1935 – Krueger's Finest beer went on sale in Richmond, Virginia.
5) Chinese astronauts
6) Viticulture
7) Snickers
8) Busking
9) Mexico
10) Moth grub moving inside the bean

Quiz 8

1) What does UNICEF stand for?
2) What country consumes the most meat per capita?
3) What continent has the largest number of Roman Catholics?
4) How many colored dots are on a Twister game mat?

5) What dog has a statue erected in Edinburgh, Scotland?

6) Before taking its current name, what company was originally called Backrub?

7) Why did pirates wear earrings?

8) What is the only miracle mentioned in all four Bible gospels?

9) What language has the most words?

10) How many people have won two Nobel Prizes?

Quiz 8 Answers

1) United Nations International Children's Emergency Fund

2) Australia

3) South America

4) 24

5) Greyfriars Bobby

6) Google

7) To improve their eyesight – They believed the precious metal in an earring had healing powers.

8) The feeding of the 5,000

9) English

10) Four – Marie Curie, Linus Pauling, John Bardeen, Frederick Sanger

Quiz 9

1) What mode of transport was invented in 1959 by the Armand Bombardier?

2) What is the name of the strong, heavy grating lowered to block the entrance to a castle?

3) What is Barbie the doll's full name?

4) What species of bird's nest is used to make bird's nest soup?

5) What modern word comes from a knight who was free for hire?

6) What is an oniomaniac obsessed with?

7) What was the first group to appear in Madame Tussauds Wax Museum as waxwork models?

8) What cosmetics giant began in 1892 as the California Perfume Company?

9) According to the Old Testament, who planted the first vineyard?

10) What country was Mother Teresa born in?

Quiz 9 Answers

1) Snowmobile

2) Portcullis

3) Barbara Millicent Roberts

4) Swift – The nest is saliva that has dried and hardened.

5) Freelance

6) Shopping

7) Beatles

8) Avon

9) Noah

10) Macedonia

Quiz 10

1) What religion was founded by Lao Tzu?

2) In what country was Greenpeace founded in 1971?

3) What year did Disneyland open?

4) What is unique about the word detartrated?

5) What is the most frequently sold item at Walmart?

6) Alfred Carlton Gilbert, a 1908 Olympic gold medal pole vaulter, invented what popular toy?

7) What is the most commonly used noun in the English language?

8) What country consumes the most fish per capita?

9) Before 1687, clocks didn't have what?

10) What person has the most statues in their honor in the U.S.?

Quiz 10 Answers

1) Taoism

2) Canada

3) 1955

4) Longest palindrome word in English – same forwards and backwards

5) Bananas

6) Erector Set

7) Time

8) Iceland

9) Minute hands

10) Sacagawea

Quiz 11

1) What does a polyandric women have more than one of?

2) In what game would you use a squidger?

3) What two cities represent letters in the phonetic alphabet?

4) As referenced in the Bible, what is myrrh?

5) If you were caught pandiculating, what were you doing?

6) What is the largest inhabited castle in the world?

7) The Clio Awards recognize achievement in what?

8) What was the first universal credit card that could be used at a variety of locations?

9) What is the oldest authenticated age ever for a human?

10) Who was the first person to speak to Jesus after he had risen from the dead?

Quiz 11 Answers

1) Husband

2) Tiddlywinks – Squidgers are the larger discs used to shoot the winks.

3) Lima and Quebec

4) A gum resin from trees

5) Stretching and stiffening your trunk and extremities as when fatigued, drowsy, or waking

6) Windsor Castle – 590,000 square feet

7) Advertising

8) Diners Club – 1950

9) 122

10) Mary Magdalene

Quiz 12

1) What did the ancient Romans throw at weddings?
2) What flavoring is added to Earl Grey tea?
3) Which of the five senses is less sharp after you eat too much?
4) What is measured on the Gay-Lussac scale?
5) What was the first patented service uniform in the U.S.?
6) What is the lowest rank of British nobility?
7) A pirate who is yelling, "Avast, ye mateys" is telling his mates to do what?
8) What country eats the most donuts per capita?
9) What country has the most vending machines per capita?
10) What did Simon of Cyrene do in the Bible?

Quiz 12 Answers

1) Walnuts – They signified hoped for fertility of bride.
2) Oil of bergamot
3) Hearing
4) Alcohol strength
5) Playboy Bunny
6) Baron
7) Stop or cease
8) Canada – The presence of 3,000 Tim Hortons restaurants is a major factor.
9) Japan – one for every 23 people
10) Carried Christ's cross

Quiz 13

1) Hotfoot Teddy was the original name of what American icon?
2) What language (not dialect) has the most characters in its alphabet?
3) What is the Decalogue more commonly known as?
4) What country has the most emigrants (people living in other countries)?

5) What is the study of word origins called?

6) Characters such as those in Chinese where a word is represented by a picture are called what?

7) What body of water is referenced in the Bible as the Great Sea?

8) In psychology, the tendency for people to believe they are above average is an effect named after what fictional town?

9) What U.S. state's constitution is the longest in the world?

10) What is a chef's hat called?

Quiz 13 Answers

1) Smokey the Bear

2) Cambodian (Khmer) – 74

3) Ten Commandments

4) Mexico

5) Etymology

6) Ideograms

7) Mediterranean Sea

8) Lake Wobegon – from Garrison Keillor's *A Prairie Home Companion*

9) Alabama – 310,000 words

10) Toque

Quiz 14

1) Who is credited with suggesting the word hello be used when answering a telephone?

2) What country has the world's oldest operating amusement park?

3) What is the button on the top of a baseball cap called?

4) For what purpose was the mouthwash Listerine originally created for?

5) What country has four of the five highest circulation newspapers in the world?

6) What element, previously used in the production of felt, led to the expression "mad as a hatter"?

7) What is coulrophobia?

8) What is the most expensive man-made object ever built?

9) What was the first car model to sell 20 million units?

10) How many possible ways are there to make change for a dollar?

Quiz 14 Answers

1) Thomas Edison – Alexander Graham Bell thought ahoy was better.

2) Denmark – 1583

3) Squatchee

4) Surgical disinfectant

5) Japan

6) Mercury – It caused poisoning.

7) Fear of clowns

8) International Space Station - $160 billion

9) Volkswagen Beetle

10) 293

Quiz 15

1) John Montagu is credited with inventing what food item?

2) How many acres in a square mile?

3) Who is the oldest man to win *People* magazine's sexiest man alive?

4) What year did the first enclosed climate-controlled mall open in the U.S.?

5) What was Play-Doh originally created for?

6) What company has been a continuous part of the Dow Jones Industrial Average stock index the longest?

7) How did the terms "upper case" and "lower case" originate regarding letters?

8) What year was the first automobile speeding ticket issued?

9) How many eyes are there in a deck of 52 cards?

10) What is the pleasant odor after a rain called?

Quiz 15 Answers

1) Sandwich – fourth Earl of Sandwich

2) 640

3) Sean Connery – 59

Miscellaneous

4) 1956 – Edina, Minnesota

5) Wallpaper cleaning putty to remove coal dust in the 1930s

6) Exxon Mobil – since 1928 as its predecessor Standard Oil of New Jersey

7) In early print shops, individual pieces of metal type were kept in boxes called cases; the smaller, more frequently used letters were kept in a lower case that was easier to reach; the less used capital letters were kept in the upper case.

8) 1896 in England - The car was going 8 mph; the speed limit for cars was 2 mph. You could go over 2 mph if you had someone walk in front of the car waving a red flag to alert people.

9) 42 – The jack of hearts, jack of spades, and king of diamonds are in profile with only one eye showing.

10) Petrichor

Quiz 16

1) What are the dots on dice called?

2) In what two countries is divorce still illegal?

3) What U.S. state has only two escalators in the entire state?

4) What is the most used letter in the English alphabet?

5) What percent alcohol is 80 proof whiskey?

6) What are the only three countries that don't use the metric system?

7) What was the original flavor of the Twinkie filling?

8) How many dots are used in each letter in the Braille system?

9) What was the first U.S. military academy to admit women?

10) What fast food franchise has the most locations worldwide?

Quiz 16 Answers

1) Pips

2) Philippines and Vatican City

3) Wyoming

4) E

5) 40%

6) United States, Liberia, Myanmar

7) Banana cream

8) Six
9) Coast Guard
10) Subway

Quiz 17

1) What year was the first published use of the word hello?
2) Kopi Luwak is a very expensive type of what?
3) What is the least used letter in the English alphabet?
4) The material that became Kleenex originally was used for what?
5) What do you call a group of unicorns?
6) What did the famous Hollywood sign in Los Angeles originally say?
7) Ferdinand Porsche designed what car launched in 1937?
8) How many witches are in a coven?
9) How did the Snickers candy bar get its name?
10) What popular soda was originally developed as a mixer for whiskey?

Quiz 17 Answers

1) 1827 – Hello is a relatively recent word and was initially used to attract attention or express surprise; it didn't get its current meaning until the telephone arrived.
2) Coffee – It is derived from partially digested coffee cherries eaten and defecated by civet cats.
3) Q
4) Gas mask filters in WWI
5) A blessing
6) Hollywoodland
7) Volkswagen Beetle
8) 13
9) Named after the creator's horse
10) Mountain Dew – 1940s

Quiz 18

1) What is the U.S. national tree?

2) Inspired by burrs, George de Mestral invented what product in the 1940s?

3) Up until 1954, what color were U.S. traffic stop signs?

4) What country has the longest constitution in the world?

5) What is the most common time to wake up in the middle of the night?

6) Why was Ted Kaczynski called the Unabomber?

7) What is rhinotillexomania?

8) What bathroom staple product was originally called Baby Gays?

9) The Vatican bank has the only ATM in the world that allows users to do what?

10) What was sex therapist Dr. Ruth trained for in the Israeli army?

Quiz 18 Answers

1) Oak

2) Velcro

3) Yellow

4) India – 146,000 words

5) 3:44 AM

6) His early targets were universities (un) and airlines (a).

7) Excessive nose picking

8) Q-tips

9) Perform transactions in Latin

10) Sniper – They thought her short stature (4'7") would make her hard to see; she had an affinity for it.

Quiz 19

1) How did the duffel bag get its name?

2) Based on enrollment, what is the largest university in the U.S.?

3) Who was the first U.S. citizen to be canonized as a saint?

4) In land surveying, how long is the chain used to measure?

5) What is a pangram?

6) Where was the highest surface wind speed ever recorded on Earth?

7) What are the monkeys Mizaru, Kikazaru, and Iwazaru better known

as?

8) Until the 1770s, what was used to erase lead pencil marks?

9) The U.S. has the most Nobel Prize winners in history; what country is second?

10) In Finland, the amount you are fined for a speeding ticket is based on what?

Quiz 19 Answers

1) Duffel, Belgium – The thick cloth used to make the bag originated there.

2) University of Central Florida

3) Mother Frances Xavier Cabrini – 1946

4) 66 feet - 10 square chains are an acre.

5) Sentence or verse that contains all letters in the alphabet at least once

6) Mount Washington, New Hampshire - 231 mph

7) See No Evil, Hear No Evil, Speak No Evil

8) Bread – decrusted, moistened and balled up

9) United Kingdom

10) Your annual income – Fines as high as 112,000 euros have been assessed.

Quiz 20

1) Since 1863, Norway has done what with all personal tax returns?

2) The U.S. has the most billionaires; what country has the second most?

3) The headquarters of Greenpeace are in what city?

4) What is the international distress signal one level less serious than Mayday?

5) In the Bible, who is Noah's grandfather?

6) What is the name for the part of a sundial that casts the shadow?

7) What is the name of the seat for riding on an elephant?

8) What is the technical name for the foam on beer?

9) Hexakosioihexekontahexaphobia is the fear of what number?

10) On a QWERTY keyboard, what two letters have raised marks to

assist with touch typing?

Quiz 20 Answers

1) Published them for everyone to see - You can see total income and total taxes for anyone; in 2014, they added the restriction that the person whose information is being requested will be notified who is looking which has resulted in far fewer inquiries.

2) China

3) Amsterdam

4) Pan-Pan

5) Methuselah – He fathered Noah's father at age 187.

6) Gnomon – from Greek meaning indicator

7) Howdah

8) Barm

9) 666

10) F and J

Quiz 21

1) If something is napiform, it is shaped like what vegetable?

2) According to the Bible, what are Adam and Eve's three named children?

3) Ahura Mazda is the sole god of what religion?

4) "March of the Volunteers" is what country's national anthem?

5) The Antoinette Perry Award for Excellence is better known as what?

6) What year was the game of Monopoly released in the U.S.?

7) When a person is micturating, what are they doing?

8) What country has the highest rate of cocaine usage?

9) It is illegal for drug companies to advertise directly to consumers almost everywhere in the world except the U.S. and what country?

10) What country has the highest number of psychiatrists per capita?

Quiz 21 Answers

1) Turnip

2) Cain, Abel, Seth

3) Zoroastrianism

4) China

5) Tony Award

6) 1935

7) Urinating

8) Scotland

9) New Zealand

10) Argentina – about six times higher than the U.S.

Quiz 22

1) U.S. television allows alcohol to be advertised if what?

2) Who manages Sweden's official Twitter account?

3) Chinese checkers originated in what country?

4) There is a cognitive bias called the cheerleader effect; what is it?

5) What is hippopotomonstrosesquippedaliophobia?

6) The word mortgage comes from a French word that means what?

7) In ancient Greece, throwing an apple at someone was a declaration of what?

8) Jesus' name translated directly from Hebrew to English would be what?

9) What is the only country that is exempt from the international rule that a country's name must appear on its postage stamps?

10) What is the most searched tutorial on YouTube?

Quiz 22 Answers

1) No alcohol is consumed in the commercial – It isn't a law or FCC regulation, just a broadcasting standard.

2) A random citizen is chosen each week to manage the account.

3) Germany – 1892

4) Bias that causes people to think that individuals are more attractive when they are in a group likely due to the averaging out of unattractive idiosyncrasies.

5) Fear of long words

6) Death contract

7) Love

8) Joshua – Jesus comes from translating Hebrew to Greek to Latin to English.

9) Great Britain – They were the first country with postage stamps and had no name on them and were exempted when the rule was made.

10) How to kiss

Quiz 23

1) What year was the company Nintendo founded?

2) Petroleum is the most valuable traded commodity; what is the second most valuable commodity?

3) What did Starbucks only sell when it started?

4) How did cappuccino get its name?

5) King Nebuchadnezzar who built the Hanging Gardens of Babylon is the best known historical sufferer of the psychological disorder boanthropy; what is boanthropy?

6) If you have a case of pronoia; what is it?

7) In 1997, Pope John Paul II nominated Saint Isidore of Seville to be the patron saint of what?

8) What country has the world's highest gambling rate?

9) Australia's first police force was composed entirely of what?

10) What is the only country in the world where more than 50% of adults have college degrees?

Quiz 23 Answers

1) 1889 – It originally produced handmade playing cards.

2) Coffee - followed by natural gas, gold, wheat

3) Whole roasted coffee beans

4) Named for the similarity of its color to the robes of the Capuchin monks

5) The sufferer believes they are a cow or ox.

6) Opposite of paranoia – feeling that a conspiracy exists to help you

7) Internet

8) Australia – Over 80% of adults gamble in some form.

9) Convicts – The best-behaved convicts were selected.

10) Canada – 51%

Quiz 24

1) What country eats the most macaroni and cheese per capita?

2) All the gold ever mined would fit in how many Olympic size swimming pools?

3) Scatomancy was popular in ancient Egypt; what is it?

4) What defines a blue moon?

5) Of the 12 men who walked on the Moon, 11 were what as children?

6) In what country did *Apollo* astronauts train because they felt it most resembled the surface of the Moon?

7) After *Apollo 11* landed on the Moon and before anyone set foot on the Moon, Buzz Aldrin did something that NASA did not want broadcast or made public, what was it?

8) What single word is the opposite of extinct?

9) How many people in modern recorded history have been struck dead by a meteorite?

10) What country has the most public holidays?

Quiz 24 Answers

1) Canada

2) Four

3) Telling the future using someone's poop

4) The second full moon in a calendar month – It happens about every three years; thus, the expression "once in a blue moon" for something that doesn't occur very often.

5) Boy Scouts

6) Iceland

7) He took communion.

8) Extant

9) One – In 2016 in India, a 40-year-old man was relaxing outside on the grounds of a small engineering college when there was the sound of an explosion; he was found next to a two-foot crater and later succumbed to injuries sustained.

10) Cambodia – 28

Quiz 25

1) Where did German chocolate cake originate?
2) What is Lake Kinneret known as in the Bible?
3) What was the earliest chocolate treat?
4) In Greek mythology, what did they believe happened to redheads when they died?
5) At what hour of the night are the most Americans sleeping?
6) At what hour of the day are the most Americans awake?
7) What letter starts the most words in the English language?
8) How many letters is the longest English word with one syllable?
9) Until the 19th century, the word hypocrites referred to what profession?
10) What is the shortest complete English sentence?

Quiz 25 Answers

1) United States – It is named after American baker Samuel German.
2) Sea of Galilee
3) Hot chocolate – Aztecs
4) They turned into vampires.
5) 3:00 AM – 95.1%
6) 6:00 PM – 97.5%
7) S
8) Nine letters – including words such as scratched, screeched, stretched, straights, strengths
9) Actors
10) Go.

Quiz 26

1) What are the three most commonly used nouns in English?
2) The word muscle comes from the Latin musculus which means what?
3) What does ambisinistrous mean?

4) The word goodbye is a contraction of what phrase?

5) The term sniper originates from what?

6) What does the word poecilonym mean?

7) What was the first country in the world to fully legalize marijuana?

8) What country has the highest percentage of marijuana users?

9) In the 19th century, doctors treated hysteria in women by inducing orgasms; what product came out of this?

10) Who coined the word makeup?

Quiz 26 Answers

1) Time, person, year

2) Little mouse – A flexed muscle was thought to resemble a mouse.

3) No good with either hand - opposite of ambidextrous

4) God be with ye.

5) How hard it is to shoot the snipe bird

6) It is a synonym for synonym.

7) Uruguay - 2013

8) Nigeria

9) Vibrator

10) Max Factor – 1920

Quiz 27

1) Where did rock paper scissors originate?

2) The word orchid is Greek and literally means what?

3) What is a sapiosexual?

4) Who is the largest retail seller of firearms in the U.S.?

5) On average, most people have fewer friends than their friends have; this is known as what?

6) What is parthenogenesis?

7) What is Captain Crunch's full name?

8) What is Minnie Mouse's full first name?

9) What does a funambulist do?

10) If you have caries, what do you have?

Quiz 27 Answers

1) China – about 2,000 years ago
2) Testicle
3) Someone who is sexually attracted to intelligence in others
4) Walmart
5) Friendship paradox – You are more likely to be friends with someone who has more friends than someone who has fewer friends.
6) Asexual reproduction – In animals, it equates to virgin birth.
7) Captain Horatio Magellan Crunch
8) Minerva
9) Tightrope walker
10) Tooth decay

Quiz 28

1) Who was Erich Weiss better known as?
2) What does a cordwainer do?
3) What English word has the most definitions?
4) What name is mentioned most in the Bible?
5) What is the world's most popular first name?
6) What job does a Foley artist do?
7) If you suffer from epistaxis, what is wrong?
8) In 1891, Whitcomb Judson invented what for fastening shoes?
9) What is the world's largest gold depository?
10) In Denmark, what is a svangerskabsforebyggendemiddel?

Quiz 28 Answers

1) Harry Houdini
2) Shoemaker – new shoes from new leather
3) Set – 464 definitions in the Oxford English dictionary
4) David – followed by Jesus
5) Mohammed and its variations
6) Sound effects

7) Nosebleed

8) Zipper

9) Manhattan Federal Reserve Bank – about 6,700 tons

10) Condom – Gummimand is the shorter, more common term.

Quiz 29

1) What poker hand is known as the dead man's hand?

2) What was first published in the *New York World* newspaper on December 21, 1913?

3) In what country did checkers originate?

4) In 1969, what category was added to the Nobel Prizes?

5) What European country's orchestra is bigger than its army?

6) Churches in Malta have two of what item to confuse the devil?

7) What Italian tractor maker first tried making cars in the 1960s?

8) What two people appeared separately on the first U.S. postage stamps issued in 1847?

9) What is the most widely used (most countries and dishes) vegetable in the world?

10) What male human feature was taxed in Elizabethan times?

Quiz 29 Answers

1) Two black aces and two black eights – This is what Wild Bill Hickok was holding when he was killed.

2) Crossword puzzle

3) Egypt – as early as 200 BC

4) Economics

5) Monaco

6) Clocks – one with the right time and one with the wrong time

7) Ferruccio Lamborghini

8) George Washington and Benjamin Franklin

9) Onion

10) Beards

Quiz 30

1) In what country did spinach originate?
2) What does ZIP stand for in ZIP code?
3) What food was invented in a sanitarium in 1894?
4) The U.S. has more airports than any other country; what country has the second most?
5) In 1829, Walter Hunt invented what common fastening item?
6) What Roman measurement is 1,500 paces?
7) Who gave the United Nations the land to build their New York headquarters?
8) What is the world's oldest monotheistic religion?
9) Dr. Ludwig Zamenhof invented what language in the 19th century?
10) What links Willy Brandt, Lech Walesa, and Yasser Arafat?

Quiz 30 Answers

1) Iran – ancient Persia
2) Zone Improvement Plan
3) Kellogg's Corn Flakes
4) Brazil - about one-third as many as the U.S.
5) Safety pin
6) League
7) John D. Rockefeller
8) Judaism
9) Esperanto
10) Nobel Peace Prize winners

Quiz 31

1) What is the name of the bridge world championship?
2) In Scrabble, what two letters are worth 10 points?
3) On a pencil, what do the initials HB stand for?
4) What is the first color mentioned in the Bible?
5) What was the first ready to eat breakfast cereal?
6) What are the four railways in the game Monopoly?

7) What is a dactylogram?
8) What are the six murder weapons in the game Clue?
9) What is the world's busiest airport based on passenger traffic?
10) What is the opposite of the Orient?

Quiz 31 Answers

1) Bermuda Bowl
2) Q and Z
3) Hard black
4) Green
5) Shredded wheat
6) Reading, Pennsylvania, B&O, Short Line
7) Fingerprint
8) Lead pipe, revolver, rope, knife, wrench, candlestick
9) Atlanta, Georgia
10) The Occident

Quiz 32

1) How many times is a Roman numeral's value increased if it has a line over it?
2) What was the first Lifesaver flavor?
3) What is the largest library in the world?
4) What soft drink first appeared in the Old Corner Drug store in Waco, Texas in 1885?
5) Who was the first American world chess champion?
6) What is the singular of graffiti?
7) What is the most widely played card game in the world?
8) What is the name of the piece flipped into the cup in tiddlywinks?
9) What is the most commonly used punctuation mark?
10) What is the most common surname in the world?

Quiz 32 Answers

1) 1,000 times
2) Peppermint

3) Library of Congress, Washington, DC
4) Dr. Pepper
5) Bobby Fischer
6) Graffito
7) Solitaire
8) Wink
9) Comma
10) Chang

Quiz 33

1) What are the three colors on a roulette wheel?
2) What letter begins the fewest words in the English language?
3) What is the middle day of a non-leap year?
4) What foreign country is visited most by Americans?
5) What was the first instant coffee?
6) What two suits have one-eyed jacks in a deck of cards?
7) What city is home to the Mayo Clinic?
8) What is AM an abbreviation for in time designations?
9) How deep is "mark twain"?
10) How many people took refuge on Noah's ark?

Quiz 33 Answers

1) Black, red, green
2) X
3) July 2
4) Mexico
5) Nescafe
6) Hearts and spades – The other suits have two-eyed jacks.
7) Rochester, Minnesota
8) Ante meridiem – meaning before noon in Latin
9) Two fathoms or twelve feet – The term was used to call out the water depth on river boats and meant mark number two for two fathoms; Samuel Clemens worked as a steamboat pilot and took his pen name from it.

10) Eight – Noah and his wife and his three sons and their wives

Quiz 34

1) What ancient measure is the distance from the elbow to the tip of the middle finger?
2) How many colored squares are there on a Rubik's cube?
3) What Hebrew word means "so be it"?
4) What was the first U.S. consumer product sold in the former Soviet Union?
5) What IQ level is the beginning of genius?
6) What is the last word of the Bible?
7) What number can't be represented in Roman numerals?
8) In terms of pounds consumed, what is the most popular vegetable in the U.S.?
9) According to the Bible, how many wise men were there?
10) What craft requires you to interlace your warp and weft?

Quiz 34 Answers

1) Cubit
2) 54
3) Amen
4) Pepsi
5) 140
6) Amen
7) Zero
8) Potato
9) It doesn't say. It says wise men and mentions the gifts; there is no indication of how many wise men.
10) Weaving

Quiz 35

1) What articles of clothing are tokens in the game Monopoly?
2) How many different calendars are needed for a perpetual calendar?
3) What word is in 1,200 different languages without changing?

4) How long after tin cans were invented was the can opener invented?

5) What is the most commonly used word in the world?

6) From what common condition would you be suffering if you had podobromhidosis?

7) Windsor Castle employs a Fendersmith; what is the job of a Fendersmith?

8) What two birds did Noah send out from the ark?

9) What word was derived from the French expression for "walking hospital"?

10) What current delicacy was served free in old west saloons to make customers drink more?

Quiz 35 Answers

1) Shoe and top hat

2) 14 – Seven for January 1 falling on each day of the week without a leap year and seven for January 1 falling on each day of the week with a leap year

3) Amen

4) 45 years

5) OK

6) Smelly feet

7) Tends and lights fires

8) Dove and raven

9) Ambulance

10) Caviar

Movies

Quiz 1

1) What well known actor made his film debut in *Critters 3* in 1991?
2) What well known actor is listed only as "stud" in the credits for *Myra Breckinridge* in 1970?
3) Who provided the demon's voice for Linda Blair's performance in *The Exorcist*?
4) What is the name of the character Dustin Hoffman plays in *Rain Man*?
5) Who directed *It's a Wonderful Life*?
6) What movie has the line "What we've got here is a failure to communicate"?
7) What was the first full length color cartoon talking picture?
8) In what movie was Bill Haley's "Rock Around the Clock" first heard?
9) In what classic western does the character Will Kane appear?
10) The song "Raindrops Keep Falling on My Head" was introduced in what movie?

Quiz 1 Answers

1) Leonardo DiCaprio
2) Tom Selleck
3) Mercedes McCambridge
4) Raymond Babbitt
5) Frank Capra
6) *Cool Hand Luke*
7) *Snow White and the Seven Dwarfs*
8) *Blackboard Jungle*
9) *High Noon*
10) *Butch Cassidy and the Sundance Kid*

Quiz 2

1) Kevin Kline won a best supporting actor Oscar for what film?
2) What 1956 film caused riots in theaters?
3) What year was *The Wizard of Oz* released?
4) What film was Kevin Costner's directorial debut?
5) What is the best-selling movie soundtrack of all time?
6) What is the name of the con that Paul Newman and Robert Redford carry out in *The Sting*?
7) How old was Shirley Temple when she made her last film?
8) What Oscar winning actress was the Connecticut state golf champion at age 16?
9) Who made her screen debut in Alfred Hitchcock's *The Trouble with Harry* in 1956?
10) What international movie star was born in a bombed out French village during WWI?

Quiz 2 Answers

1) *A Fish Called Wanda*
2) *Rock Around the Clock*
3) 1939
4) *Dances with Wolves*
5) *The Bodyguard*
6) The wire
7) 22
8) Katharine Hepburn
9) Shirley MacLaine
10) Rin Tin Tin

Quiz 3

1) What is the name of the character played by John Wayne in *The Quiet Man*?
2) Who played the ballet teacher in *Billy Elliot*?
3) What is the name of the police character played by Roy Scheider in *Jaws*?

4) For what film did Frank Sinatra win his only acting Oscar?

5) In the James Bond movies, who is the only actress to play Bond's wife?

6) In what film did Alec Guinness play eight parts?

7) What actor had the male lead in Hitchcock's *The Birds*?

8) Who was the actress sister of Olivia de Havilland?

9) What actor died during the filming of *Gladiator*?

10) What actor led *The Dirty Dozen*?

Quiz 3 Answers

1) Sean Thornton

2) Julie Walters

3) Martin Brody

4) *From Here to Eternity*

5) Diana Rigg – *On Her Majesty's Secret Service*

6) *Kind Hearts and Coronets*

7) Rod Taylor

8) Joan Fontaine

9) Oliver Reed

10) Lee Marvin

Quiz 4

1) In *Star Wars*, what is the name of Princess Leia's home planet?

2) Who won a best actor Oscar for *Marty*?

3) Prior to *Schindler's List* in 1993, what was the last black and white movie to win the best picture Oscar?

4) What is the name of Michael Douglas' character in *Wall Street*?

5) For what 1974 film did Art Carney win a best actor Oscar?

6) What character has been portrayed by Reginald Owen, Alistair Sim, and Albert Finney?

7) For what film did Burl Ives win a best supporting actor Oscar?

8) Who was the first film star to earn 1 million dollars for a single film?

9) Who made his film debut as Boo Radley in *To Kill a Mockingbird*?

10) What was Marilyn Monroe's last film?

Quiz 4 Answers

1) Alderaan
2) Ernest Borgnine
3) *The Apartment* – 1960
4) Gordon Gekko
5) *Harry and Tonto*
6) Ebenezer Scrooge
7) *The Big Country*
8) Elizabeth Taylor – *Cleopatra* in 1963
9) Robert Duvall
10) *The Misfits*

Quiz 5

1) What year was Clint Eastwood's first spaghetti western made?
2) What movie cast included James Garner, Steve McQueen, Charles Bronson, Donald Pleasance, and James Coburn?
3) What musical won the best picture Oscar in 1968?
4) What is the name of Audrey Hepburn's character in *Breakfast at Tiffany's*?
5) Who played James Bond in the 1966 film *Casino Royale*?
6) Who was voted most popular film performer in the U.S. in 1926?
7) What was Vincent Price's last film?
8) How old was Orson Welles when he co-wrote, produced, directed and starred in *Citizen Kane*?
9) Who played the two crooks in *Home Alone*?
10) Who did Sergio Leone originally want to play the lead in *A Fistful of Dollars* but couldn't afford his salary?

Quiz 5 Answers

1) 1964
2) *The Great Escape*
3) *Oliver!*

4) Holly Golightly

5) David Niven

6) Rin Tin Tin

7) *Edward Scissorhands* – 1990

8) 25

9) Daniel Stern and Joe Pesci

10) Henry Fonda – Many actors turned down the role before Clint Eastwood accepted and was paid $15,000 for the role.

Quiz 6

1) What is the only movie Alfred Hitchcock made twice?

2) Who is Melanie Griffith's mother?

3) What character did Michael J. Fox play in *Back to the Future*?

4) What film followed the career of athletes Eric Henry Liddell and Harold Abrahams?

5) Set in a Los Angeles office building, the 1979 novel *Nothing Lasts Forever* is the basis for what film?

6) In what film does a disturbed romance novel enthusiast gush, "I am your number one fan"?

7) Who was the first choice to play Indiana Jones but missed out due to other commitments?

8) Who is Ben Hur's rival in the great chariot race?

9) What Marlon Brando film was widely banned?

10) What was the last of the five Dirty Harry movies?

Quiz 6 Answers

1) *The Man Who Knew Too Much* – 1934 and 1956

2) Tippi Hedren – star of Alfred Hitchcock's *The Birds*

3) Marty McFly

4) *Chariots of Fire*

5) *Die Hard*

6) *Misery*

7) Tom Selleck

8) Messala

9) *Last Tango in Paris*
10) *The Dead Pool*

Quiz 7

1) In what movie did Hugh Grant play the role of the British Prime Minister?
2) Who was the first non-British act to perform a James Bond movie theme song?
3) What character sang "When You Wish Upon a Star" in Disney's *Pinocchio*?
4) "The Windmills of Your Mind" is the theme song for what 1968 film?
5) In *Home Alone*, what is the first name of Macaulay Culkin's character?
6) What is the name of Jeff Bridge's character in *The Big Lebowski*?
7) The Olympics depicted in *Chariots of Fire* took place in what year?
8) Who played Freddy Krueger in the *Nightmare on Elm Street* films?
9) Lee Marvin won the best actor Oscar for what 1965 film?
10) What actor is stung in *The Sting*?

Quiz 7 Answers

1) *Love Actually*
2) Nancy Sinatra - *You Only Live Twice*
3) Jiminy Cricket
4) *The Thomas Crown Affair*
5) Kevin
6) The Dude or Jeff Lebowski
7) 1924
8) Robert Englund
9) *Cat Ballou*
10) Robert Shaw

Quiz 8

1) For what movie did Rod Steiger win a best actor Oscar?

2) What was the top grossing U.S. film of the 1960s?

3) What was Spencer Tracey and Katharine Hepburn's first film in 1942?

4) What comedy ended with the line "Hey, can I try on your yellow dress?"

5) What is the name of the dog owned by Nick and Nora Charles in *The Thin Man*?

6) What character did Mel Gibson play in *Braveheart*?

7) Gene Hackman received an Oscar for his portrayal of the sheriff of Big Whiskey in what movie?

8) What book does Forrest Gump keep in his suitcase?

9) What is Joy Adamson's lion cub called in *Born Free*?

10) What is the name of Kurt Russell's character in *Escape from New York*?

Quiz 8 Answers

1) *In the Heat of the Night*
2) *The Sound of Music*
3) *Woman of the Year*
4) *Tootsie*
5) Asta
6) William Wallace
7) *Unforgiven*
8) *Curious George*
9) Elsa
10) Snake Plissken

Quiz 9

1) Who played Lois Lane in 1978's *Superman*?
2) What film has the line "I coulda been a contender"?
3) Who played Miss Hannigan in 1982's *Annie*?
4) What is the name of the serial killer in *Halloween*?
5) Who is the youngest actor ever nominated for an Oscar?
6) Who played Anna in 1956's *The King and I*?

7) Who directed *Blade Runner*?

8) Who played Beau Geste in the 1939 film?

9) *Bambi* was the first Disney film without what?

10) What is the only movie character that has won Oscars for two different actors?

Quiz 9 Answers

1) Margot Kidder

2) *On the Waterfront*

3) Carol Burnett

4) Michael Myers

5) Justin Henry – eight years old for *Kramer vs. Kramer*

6) Deborah Kerr

7) Ridley Scott

8) Gary Cooper

9) Human characters

10) Vito Corleone – Marlon Brando and Robert de Niro in *The Godfather* and *The Godfather Part II*

Quiz 10

1) What 1948 classic film was advertised as "Greed, gold and gunplay on a Mexican mountain of malice"?

2) What is the name of Kevin Costner's character in *Field of Dreams*?

3) Who played the part of Cruella de Vil in 1996's *101 Dalmatians*?

4) What was the sequel to *Going My Way*?

5) Who played Dr. Frankenfurter in *The Rocky Horror Picture Show*?

6) What was Spencer Tracy's last film?

7) What film has the insult "Your mother was a hamster, and your father smelt of elderberries"?

8) In what 1976 film is the lead character asked repeatedly "Is it safe?"

9) Elvis Presley memorized every line from his all-time favorite movie; what was the film?

10) What cartoon duo has won seven Oscars for best animated short film?

Quiz 10 Answers

1) *The Treasure of the Sierra Madre*
2) Ray Kinsella
3) Glenn Close
4) *The Bells of St. Mary's*
5) Tim Curry
6) *Guess Who's Coming to Dinner*
7) *Monty Python and the Holy Grail*
8) *Marathon Man*
9) *Patton*
10) Tom and Jerry

Quiz 11

1) The character Marion Crane died famously in what film?
2) Marnie Nixon did what for Deborah Kerr, Natalie Wood, and Audrey Hepburn?
3) What is the name of Gene Hackman's character in *The French Connection*?
4) Who played Norman Bates in *Psycho*?
5) What was the first Disney animated film based on the life of a real person?
6) What romantic comedy has the line "I'll have what she's having"?
7) What is the name of the witch in Disney's *Sleeping Beauty*?
8) What film is set in and around 17 Cherry Tree Lane, London in 1910?
9) What was the first Andrew Lloyd Webber musical to be filmed?
10) What is the name of Bill Murray's character in *Ghostbusters*?

Quiz 11 Answers

1) *Psycho* – shower scene
2) Dubbed their singing voices
3) Popeye Doyle
4) Anthony Perkins

5) *Pocahontas*

6) *When Harry Met Sally*

7) Maleficent

8) *Mary Poppins*

9) *Jesus Christ Superstar*

10) Peter Venkman

Quiz 12

1) In what Hitchcock film does Doris Day sing the Oscar winning song "Que Sera, Sera"?

2) What 1969 western won best story and best song Oscars?

3) "Somewhere My Love" is the theme song of what movie?

4) What character is the heroine of *The Silence of the Lambs*?

5) What actor is in both *The Magnificent Seven* and *The Dirty Dozen*?

6) Who was the first actor to receive a posthumous Oscar nomination?

7) What movie has the line "You're gonna need a bigger boat"?

8) What 1954 film won eight Oscars?

9) What are James Dean's three films?

10) Who were the first father and son to win Oscars for the same film?

Quiz 12 Answers

1) *The Man Who Knew Too Much*

2) *Butch Cassidy and the Sundance Kid*

3) *Doctor Zhivago*

4) Clarice Starling

5) Charles Bronson

6) James Dean – *East of Eden* in 1956

7) *Jaws*

8) *On the Waterfront*

9) *Rebel Without a Cause, East of Eden, Giant*

10) Walter and John Huston – *The Treasure of the Sierra Madre*

Quiz 13

1) What actor said, "Love means never having to say you're sorry"?
2) What actor rode the bomb down in *Dr. Strangelove*?
3) Who played Commodious in *Gladiator*?
4) In what movie did Bruce Willis play Korben Dallas?
5) Linda Hunt won an Oscar for *The Year of Living Dangerously*; it was the first Oscar for what?
6) What does the C stand for in George C. Scott?
7) What was the world's first X-rated cartoon?
8) The Oscar winning 1968 movie *Charly* is based on what novel?
9) What newspaper owner's career inspired *Citizen Kane*?
10) What film produced the first female best director Oscar?

Quiz 13 Answers

1) Ryan O'Neil
2) Slim Pickens
3) Joaquin Phoenix
4) *The Fifth Element*
5) Playing the opposite sex
6) Campbell
7) *Fritz the Cat* – 1972
8) *Flowers for Algernon*
9) William Randolph Hearst
10) *The Hurt Locker* – Kathryn Bigelow

Quiz 14

1) Who played the role of Mrs. Robinson in *The Graduate*?
2) Who is the oldest best actress Oscar winner?
3) Who is the oldest best actor Oscar winner?
4) "Well, nobody's perfect!" is the last line of what comedy?
5) What is the name of Dustin Hoffman's character in *The Graduate*?
6) What 1957 film took place in 1943 Burma?
7) In what film did Paul Newman's character eat 50 hard-boiled eggs?

8) For what film did James Cagney win his only Oscar?

9) What was Charles Foster Kane's dying word?

10) For what 1955 film did Jack Lemon win his first Oscar?

Quiz 14 Answers

1) Anne Bancroft

2) Jessica Tandy – 80 for *Driving Miss Daisy*

3) Henry Fonda – 76 for *On Golden Pond*

4) *Some Like It Hot*

5) Benjamin Braddock

6) *The Bridge on the River Kwai*

7) *Cool Hand Luke*

8) *Yankee Doodle Dandy*

9) Rosebud

10) *Mister Roberts*

Quiz 15

1) Who won a best actor Oscar for *Amadeus*?

2) Who played the sleuthing couple in the *Thin Man* series of films?

3) In what film did Orson Welles play the character Harry Lime?

4) What three counties is Eliza Doolittle taught to pronounce in *My Fair Lady*?

5) What is the name of Humphrey Bogart's character in *The African Queen*?

6) What actor starred in both Alfred Hitchcock's *Rope* and *Strangers on a Train*?

7) Packy East, an amateur boxer, became famous as a comedian under what name?

8) What film featured Rosie O'Donnell, Rita Wilson, and Meg Ryan?

9) What is the name of Sigourney Weaver's character in *Alien*?

10) What mythical Scottish town appears for one day every hundred years?

Quiz 15 Answers

1) F. Murray Abraham
2) William Powell and Myrna Loy
3) *The Third Man*
4) Hertford, Hereford, Hampshire
5) Charlie Allnut
6) Farley Granger
7) Bob Hope
8) *Sleepless in Seattle*
9) Ellen Ripley
10) Brigadoon

Quiz 16

1) *The Wizard of Oz* lost the best picture Oscar to what movie?
2) What are the only two best picture Oscar winning films that were based on best musical Tony Award winners?
3) What 1979 film has a spaceship named Nostromo?
4) What movie sold the most tickets of all time in the U.S.?
5) What movie starred Lee Marvin as twins Kid Shelleen and Tim Strawn?
6) In *Back to the Future*, how fast does the DeLorean have to go to time travel?
7) What was the first comedy to win the best picture Oscar?
8) Who was the first actor to direct himself to a best actor Oscar?
9) Robin Williams won a best supporting actor Oscar for what film?
10) What famous actor made his film debut in *A Nightmare on Elm Street*?

Quiz 16 Answers

1) *Gone with the Wind*
2) *My Fair Lady* and *The Sound of Music*
3) *Alien*
4) *Gone with the Wind* – About 208 million tickets have been sold; the U.S. population in 1939 when it was released was 131 million.

5) *Cat Ballou*

6) 88 mph

7) *It Happened One Night* – 1934

8) Laurence Olivier – *Hamlet* in 1948

9) *Good Will Hunting*

10) Johnny Depp

Quiz 17

1) What three sports related movies have won the best picture Oscar?

2) What is Dorothy's last name in *The Wizard of Oz*?

3) Adjusted for inflation, what is the highest grossing U.S. movie of all time?

4) What is the lowest grossing film to ever win the best picture Oscar?

5) What was the first animated film nominated for the best picture Oscar?

6) What was the first movie from a non-English speaking country to win the best picture Oscar?

7) What best picture Oscar nominee used the "F" word the most times?

8) What was Elvis Presley's last movie?

9) What was the first foreign film to win the best picture Oscar?

10) What is the highest grossing romantic comedy film of all time?

Quiz 17 Answers

1) *Rocky, Chariots of Fire, Million Dollar Baby*

2) Gale

3) *Gone with the Wind* – followed by *Star Wars* and *The Sound of Music*

4) *The Hurt Locker* – 2008

5) *Beauty and the Beast* – 1991

6) *The Artist* – France in 2011

7) *The Wolf of Wall Street* – more than 500 times

8) *Change of Habit* – 1969 with Mary Tyler Moore

9) *Hamlet* – 1948

10) *My Big Fat Greek Wedding*

Quiz 18

1) What famous actor competed in the 1953 Mr. Universe bodybuilding competition?
2) What is the first R-rated movie to win the best picture Oscar?
3) What is the first horror film nominated for the best picture Oscar?
4) Who is the only person to write back to back best picture Oscar winners?
5) What male actor has the most Oscar nominations?
6) What is the only X-rated movie to win the best picture Oscar?
7) What was the first movie to make $100 million at the box office?
8) Who is the youngest Oscar winner ever?
9) Who played James Bond in *On Her Majesty's Secret Service* in 1969?
10) What was the first western to win the best picture Oscar?

Quiz 18 Answers

1) Sean Connery
2) *The French Connection*
3) *The Exorcist* – 1973
4) Paul Haggis – *Million Dollar Baby* and *Crash*
5) Jack Nicholson
6) *Midnight Cowboy* – It was X-rated at the time of the award; in 1971, its rating was changed to R.
7) *Jaws*
8) Tatum O'Neal – 10 years old for *Paper Moon*
9) George Lazenby
10) *Cimarron* – 1931

Quiz 19

1) What country has won the foreign language Oscar the most times?
2) What was Alfred Hitchcock's only best picture Oscar winner?
3) What are the only two Pulitzer Prize winning novels to be made into Oscar best picture winners?
4) What is the first and only G-rated movie to win the best picture Oscar?

5) What was the first film to win the Oscar for best animated feature?

6) What was the first sports film to win the best picture Oscar?

7) What is the longest movie to ever win the best picture Oscar?

8) Who is the only author to have his works simultaneously number one in television, film, and books?

9) What actor has the most Oscar nominations without a win?

10) What was John Wayne's last movie?

Quiz 19 Answers

1) Italy

2) *Rebecca* – 1940

3) *Gone with the Wind* and *All the King's Men*

4) *Oliver!*

5) *Shrek*

6) *Rocky* – 1976

7) *Gone with the Wind* - 238 minutes

8) Michael Crichton – *ER* (television), *Jurassic Park* (film), *Disclosure* (book)

9) Peter O'Toole – eight

10) *The Shootist*

Quiz 20

1) Bruce Willis played a time traveler in what 1995 movie?

2) What is the only film based on a television show to win the best picture Oscar?

3) Who are the two actors who get stuck traveling together in *Planes, Trains and Automobiles*?

4) What are the only three films to win all five major Academy Awards (best picture, director, actor, actress, screenplay)?

5) What is the only fantasy film to win the best picture Oscar?

6) What was the first U.S. film with a female director to gross over $100 million?

7) What is the name of the giant bird in *Up*?

8) What is the name of the skunk in Disney's *Bambi*?

9) What was the first feature film broadcast on U.S. television?

10) What was the first full color film to win the best picture Oscar?

Quiz 20 Answers

1) *12 Monkeys*

2) *Marty* – 1955

3) Steve Martin and John Candy

4) *It Happened One Night* (1934), *One Flew Over the Cuckoo's Nest* (1975), *The Silence of the Lambs* (1991)

5) *The Lord of the Rings: The Return of the King* – 2003

6) *Big* – directed by Penny Marshall in 1988

7) Kevin

8) Flower

9) *The Wizard of Oz* – broadcast in 1956

10) *Gone with the Wind*

Quiz 21

1) What are the only two sequels to win best picture Oscars?

2) Who is the only Oscar winner whose parents were both Oscar winners?

3) Who are the only brothers to receive acting Oscar nominations?

4) What two western movies won best picture Oscars in the 1990s?

5) Who are the only brother and sister to win acting Oscars?

6) What two families have three generations of Oscar winners?

7) Who is the only person named Oscar to win an Oscar?

8) Who is the only actor to appear in multiple films and have every one nominated for the best picture Oscar?

9) What was the screen name of Lee Yuen Kam?

10) For what 1971 film did Jane Fonda win her first Oscar?

Quiz 21 Answers

1) *The Godfather Part II* and *The Lord of the Rings: The Return of the King*

2) Liza Minnelli

3) River and Joaquin Phoenix

4) *Dances with Wolves* and *Unforgiven*

5) Lionel and Ethel Barrymore

6) Huston (Walter, John, and Anjelica) and Coppola (Carmine, Francis Ford, and Sofia)

7) Oscar Hammerstein II

8) John Cazale – He appeared in *The Godfather*, *The Conversation*, *The Godfather Part II*, *Dog Day Afternoon*, and *The Deer Hunter*.

9) Bruce Lee

10) *Klute*

Quiz 22

1) What was the screen name of Edda Van Heemstra?

2) Who is the only person with four acting Oscars?

3) Who dubbed Miss Piggy's singing voice in *The Muppet Movie*?

4) What was Disney's first live action feature movie?

5) For what film did Steven Spielberg win his first Oscar?

6) What movie has the line "I love the smell of napalm in the morning"?

7) "I'm mad as hell, and I'm not going to take this anymore!" is a line from what movie?

8) Sterling Holloway was the original voice of what Disney character?

9) What is the name of the character Sidney Poitier played in *Lilies of the Field*?

10) What three films are tied for the most Oscars at 11 each?

Quiz 22 Answers

1) Audrey Hepburn

2) Katharine Hepburn

3) Johnny Mathis

4) *Treasure Island*

5) *Schindler's List*

6) *Apocalypse Now*

7) *Network*

8) Winnie the Pooh

9) Homer Smith

10) *Ben-Hur, Titanic, The Lord of the Rings: The Return of the King*

Quiz 23

1) What woman has won the most Oscars?

2) Who are the only two actresses who have won consecutive best actress Oscars?

3) Who are the only two actors who have won consecutive best actor Oscars?

4) For what movie did the first woman win a best picture Oscar?

5) What actor has appeared in the most best picture Oscar winning movies?

6) What 1985 western starred Kevin Kline, Danny Glover, Kevin Costner, John Cleese, Jeff Goldblum, and Linda Hunt?

7) What is the first name of Dustin Hoffman's female character in *Tootsie*?

8) What is the day job of Jennifer Beale's character in *Flashdance*?

9) In what film did Sean Connery play James Bond after a 12-year absence?

10) Who spoke the only word in Mel Brooks' *Silent Movie*?

Quiz 23 Answers

1) Edith Head – eight for costume design

2) Luise Rainer – *The Great Ziegfeld* (1936) and *The Good Earth* (1937) and Katharine Hepburn – *Guess Who's Coming to Dinner* (1967) and *The Lion in Winter* (1968)

3) Spencer Tracy – *Captains Courageous* (1937) and *Boys Town* (1938) and Tom Hanks – *Philadelphia* (1993) and *Forrest Gump* (1994)

4) *The Sting* – 1973

5) Franklyn Farnum – He was a character actor in 433 films including seven best picture winners – *The Life of Emile Zola* (1937), *Going My Way* (1944), *The Lost Weekend* (1945), *Gentleman's Agreement* (1947), *All About Eve* (1950), *The Greatest Show on Earth* (1952), and *Around the World in 80 Says* (1956).

6) *Silverado*

7) Dorothy

8) Welder
9) *Never Say Never Again*
10) Marcel Marceau – French mime

Quiz 24

1) Who played Elliot Ness in *The Untouchables*?
2) Who played Louise in *Thelma and Louise*?
3) What is the name of Kevin Spacey's character in *The Usual Suspects*?
4) Who played Dr. Strangelove?
5) What is the name of Jack Nicholson's character in *Chinatown*?
6) Who played Mozart in *Amadeus*?
7) What 1953 western starred Alan Ladd, Jean Arthur, and Van Heflin?
8) What was the first feature film with Tom Hanks and Meg Ryan?
9) Who said during their one and only Oscar acceptance speech, "I think they gave it to me because I'm the oldest"?
10) Who directed *The Bridge on the River Kwai*?

Quiz 24 Answers

1) Kevin Costner
2) Susan Sarandon
3) Keyser Soze or Roger "Verbal" Kint
4) Peter Sellers
5) Jake Gittes
6) Tom Hulce
7) *Shane*
8) *Joe Versus the Volcano*
9) Jessica Tandy – 80 at the time
10) David Lean

Quiz 25

1) What is the real name of superhero Iron Man?
2) What was the last animated film personally supervised by Walt Disney?
3) What is Carrie's last name in *Carrie*?

4) For what film did Audrey Hepburn win her only Oscar?

5) Who played Rooster Cogburn in the 2010 *True Grit remake*?

6) What is the highest grossing hand drawn animated film in history?

7) What character did Louise Fletcher play in *One Flew over the Cuckoo's Nest*?

8) What 1990 movie was the first western to win the best picture Oscar in 59 years?

9) Who was the first actress to win an Oscar for a performance entirely in a foreign language?

10) Who played the title roles in 1977's *Fun with Dick and Jane*?

Quiz 25 Answers

1) Anthony Stark

2) *The Jungle Book* – 1967

3) White

4) *Roman Holiday*

5) Jeff Bridges

6) *The Lion King*

7) Nurse Ratched

8) *Dances with Wolves*

9) Sophia Loren - 1962

10) George Segal and Jane Fonda

Quiz 26

1) What is the title of the sequel to *Romancing the Stone*?

2) *The Magnificent Seven* is based on what 1954 film?

3) Heath Ledger and Jake Gyllenhaal play sheep herders in what film?

4) In what 1968 film did Benny Hill play a toymaker?

5) What song in 1981's *Arthur* won an Oscar?

6) Who is the arch enemy of Austin Powers?

7) In *The Hunger Games*, what is the name of the futuristic nation?

8) What are the first names of the film making Coen brothers?

9) In the James Bond films, what does the acronym SPECTRE stand for?

10) What science fiction movie was originally made in 1956 and remade in 1978 and 1993?

Quiz 26 Answers

1) *The Jewel of the Nile*

2) *Seven Samurai*

3) *Brokeback Mountain*

4) *Chitty Chitty Bang Bang*

5) "Best That You Can Do"

6) Dr. Evil

7) Panem

8) Joel and Ethan

9) Special Executive for Counterintelligence Terror Revenge and Extortion

10) *Invasion of the Body Snatchers*

Quiz 27

1) Meryl Streep and Dustin Hoffman played husband and wife in what movie?

2) In the *Lethal Weapon* movies, what is Mel Gibson's character name?

3) What three actors played *The Good, The Bad, and The Ugly*?

4) What is the name of John Travolta's character in *Grease*?

5) Who is the only person with a star in each of the five categories (movies, television, music, radio, and live performance) on the Hollywood Walk of Fame?

6) In what Alfred Hitchcock film did Julie Andrews star with Paul Newman?

7) What is Bill Murray's character name in *Caddyshack*?

8) In Disney's *Snow White and the Seven Dwarfs*, what do the dwarfs mine?

9) What film is based on the Stephen King novella *The Body*?

10) Timothy Q. Mouse, Mr. Stork and Jim Crow are characters in what Disney film?

Quiz 27 Answers

1) *Kramer vs Kramer*
2) Martin Riggs
3) Clint Eastwood, Lee Van Cleef, Eli Wallach
4) Danny Zuko
5) Gene Autry
6) *Torn Curtain*
7) Carl Spackler
8) Diamonds
9) *Stand by Me*
10) *Dumbo*

Quiz 28

1) Who is the youngest best actress Oscar winner?
2) Who is the youngest best actor Oscar winner?
3) Who has the most acting Oscar nominations?
4) What actor or actress has the longest time between their first and last Oscars?
5) What two actresses tied for the 1968 best actress Oscar?
6) Who is the only person to win the best actor Oscar three times?
7) Who played Danny Ocean in 1960's *Ocean's 11*?
8) In *Ben-Hur*, what is the title character's first name?
9) Contractually, who had to be first offered the role of John McClane in *Die Hard*?
10) What is Richard Gere's middle name?

Quiz 28 Answers

1) Marlee Matlin – 21 for *Children of a Lesser God*
2) Adrien Brody – 29 for *The Pianist*
3) Meryl Streep
4) Katharine Hepburn – 48 years from 1933 to 1981
5) Barbra Streisand (*Funny Girl*) and Katharine Hepburn (*The Lion in Winter*)

6) Daniel Day-Lewis – *My Left Foot, There Will Be Blood, Lincoln*

7) Frank Sinatra

8) Judah

9) Frank Sinatra – He was 73 at the time. The movie is based on the book *Nothing Lasts Forever* which was a sequel to *The Detective* which had been made into a movie in 1968 starring Sinatra; contractually, he had to be offered the role first.

10) Tiffany

Quiz 29

1) In the original script for *Back to the Future*, the time machine wasn't a DeLorean; what was it?

2) The U.S. film industry relocated from New York to Los Angeles in large part because of what man?

3) During filming of *The Blues Brothers*, they had a special budget for what during night shoots?

4) The "no animals were harmed" statement on movies only applies when?

5) After dropping out 34 years earlier, Steven Spielberg got his Bachelor of Arts degree from Cal State Long Beach; what did he submit for credit for his final project in advanced film making?

6) What movie has the highest number of on screen deaths of all time?

7) What actor has died the most times on screen?

8) Who was the inspiration for the character of Biff Tannen, the bully in *Back to the Future*?

9) The Tom Hanks movie *The Terminal* was inspired by a man who lived at the departure lounge of what international airport for 18 years?

10) The first Cannes Film Festival was called off after screening only one film; why?

Quiz 29 Answers

1) Refrigerator

2) Thomas Edison – He held many of the patents on the production and showing of movies and controlled the industry; film makers escaped to Los Angeles to get away from his control.

3) Cocaine

4) While film is recording

5) *Schindler's List*

6) *The Lord of the Rings: The Return of the King* – 836 deaths

7) John Hurt – 43 times including *Alien*, *Spaceballs*, *V for Vendetta*, *Hellboy*

8) Donald Trump

9) Charles de Gaulle Airport

10) WWII broke out.

Quiz 30

1) In Disney's *Snow White and the Seven Dwarfs*, how old is Snow White?

2) Who is the first person to have the number one movie and record album in the same week?

3) Michael Jackson wanted to buy Marvel Comics; what was his primary motive?

4) "Badges? We ain't got no badges! We don't need no badges! I don't have to show you any stinking badges!" is from what film?

5) Why wasn't the original *Tron* movie in 1982 considered for a visual effects Oscar?

6) What year did the first screen kiss between two men occur?

7) Sylvester Stallone was so poor at one point that he sold something he loved for $50 only to buy it back for $3,000 one week later when he sold the script for Rocky; what was it?

8) What was the first Disney animated feature film set in America?

9) What individual has won the most Oscar awards?

10) What was the first film Clint Eastwood directed?

Quiz 30 Answers

1) 14

2) Jennifer Lopez – 2001

3) He wanted to play Spider Man in his own movie.

4) *The Treasure of the Sierra Madre*

5) The Academy felt the filmmakers had cheated by using computers.

6) 1927 – *Wings*
7) **His dog**
8) *Dumbo*
9) Walt Disney – 22 competitive and 4 honorary awards
10) *Play Misty for Me*

Quiz 31

1) Who did Michael Caine play in *The Ipcress File*?
2) Who played the scarecrow in *The Wizard of Oz*?
3) What was the first James Bond film?
4) In movie making, what job does the gaffer do?
5) What actor has been portrayed most on the screen by other actors?
6) Who directed *Dr. Strangelove* and *2001: A Space Odyssey*?
7) In what Alfred Hitchcock film does he make his usual appearance in a newspaper weight loss ad?
8) What country made the world's first feature film in 1906?
9) What is Norman Bates' hobby in *Psycho*?
10) What real person has been played most often in films?

Quiz 31 Answers

1) Harry Palmer
2) Ray Bolger
3) *Dr. No*
4) Chief electrician
5) Charlie Chaplin
6) Stanley Kubrick
7) *Lifeboat* – Due to the setting in a lifeboat, he couldn't make his usual in person cameo appearance.
8) Australia
9) Stuffing birds
10) Napoleon Bonaparte

Quiz 32

1) Humphrey Bogart starred in the first film John Huston directed;

what was it?

2) What film star was the first to appear on a postage stamp?

3) Who did Babe the pig work for?

4) Shirley Bassey sang the theme song for which three Bond films?

5) Anthony Daniels played what character in a series of films?

6) Who was the first actor to appear on the cover of *Time* magazine?

7) Who played the title role in *Lawrence of Arabia*?

8) What 1942 Humphrey Bogart film won the best picture Oscar?

9) What country makes the most films per year?

10) Who built the world's first film studio?

Quiz 32 Answers

1) *The Maltese Falcon*

2) Grace Kelly

3) Farmer Hoggett

4) *Goldfinger, Diamonds Are Forever, Moonraker*

5) C-3PO - *Star Wars*

6) Charlie Chaplin

7) Peter O'Toole

8) *Casablanca*

9) India

10) Thomas Edison

Quiz 33

1) What actor played Wyatt Earp, Frank James, and Abraham Lincoln?

2) In 1944's *National Velvet*, what is the name of Velvet Brown's horse?

3) Who played the Cooler King in *The Great Escape*?

4) What two films did Paul Newman play Fast Eddie Felson in?

5) What is the theme song for *The Grapes of Wrath*?

6) How many Oscars did *Gone with the Wind* win?

7) Who played Tarzan in more movies than anyone else?

8) What actors were chained together in 1958's *The Defiant Ones*?

9) What two child actors co-starred in the first Lassie movie?

10) Who did Gregory Peck portray in *The Boys from Brazil*?

Quiz 33 Answers

1) Henry Fonda
2) The Pie
3) Steve McQueen
4) *The Hustler* and *The Color of Money*
5) "The Red River Valley"
6) Nine
7) Johnny Weissmuller
8) Tony Curtis and Sidney Poitier
9) Roddy McDowall and Elizabeth Taylor
10) Dr. Josef Mengele

Quiz 34

1) What is the name of Jimmy Stewart's character in *It's a Wonderful Life*?
2) For what film did Sidney Poitier win a best actor Oscar?
3) Who played Christ in *The Greatest Story Ever Told*?
4) What is the name of the island that is King Kong's home?
5) Who played the cowardly lion in *The Wizard of Oz*?
6) What 1941 portrayal won Gary Cooper a best actor Oscar?
7) What is the name of Marlon Brando's character in *A Streetcar Named Desire*?
8) What movie has the tiny country of Grand Fenwick declaring war on the U.S.?
9) What is the name of the Tennessee sheriff played by Joe Don Baker in *Walking Tall*?
10) What is the theme song for *Midnight Cowboy*?

Quiz 34 Answers

1) George Bailey
2) *Lilies of the Field*
3) Max Von Sydow

4) Skull Island
5) Bert Lahr
6) Sergeant Alvin York
7) Stanley Kowalski
8) *The Mouse That Roared*
9) Buford Pusser
10) "Everybody's Talkin'"

Quiz 35

1) What is Dirty Harry's last name?
2) What pool shark did Jackie Gleason play in *The Hustler*?
3) Who played the demolitions expert in *The Guns of Navarone*?
4) Who is Goldfinger's bodyguard?
5) For what film did Louise Fletcher win a best actress Oscar?
6) What film made Hattie McDaniel the first African American Oscar winner?
7) What was Judy Garland's real name?
8) Who were the five Marx brothers?
9) What film dramatized the Scopes Monkey Trial?
10) What judge did Walter Brennan, Edgar Buchanan, and Paul Newman all portray?

Quiz 35 Answers

1) Callahan
2) Minnesota Fats
3) David Niven
4) Oddjob
5) *One Flew Over the Cuckoo's Nest*
6) *Gone with the Wind*
7) Frances Gumm
8) Groucho, Chico, Harpo, Zeppo, Gummo
9) *Inherit the Wind*
10) Roy Bean

Quiz 36

1) Which of the seven dwarfs comes first alphabetically?
2) What city is the setting for *Chinatown*?
3) Who were the two stars in the original *Sleuth*?
4) What was the first talking motion picture with the sound in the film?
5) Who played Helen Keller in *The Miracle Worker*?
6) Spencer Tracy played the father in *Father of the Bride*; who played the bride?
7) Who won a best actor Oscar for *Network*?
8) For what 1960 role did Burt Lancaster win a best actor Oscar?
9) What is the name of Sean Penn's character in *Fast Times at Ridgemont High*?
10) What actor provided the voice for Francis the talking mule?

Quiz 36 Answers

1) Bashful
2) Los Angeles
3) Laurence Olivier and Michael Caine
4) *The Jazz Singer* – 1927
5) Patty Duke
6) Elizabeth Taylor
7) Peter Finch
8) Elmer Gantry
9) Jeff Spicoli
10) Chill Wills

Quiz 37

1) What actor is often credited with saving Warner Brothers Studio from bankruptcy and received the most votes for the best actor Oscar at the first Academy Awards in 1929 before being eliminated from the ballot?
2) What 1963 comedy had more than 50 stars in it?
3) Who is the only person to win Oscars for best actress and best

song?

4) What did Cool Hand Luke go to jail for?

5) Who played sidekick to Hopalong Cassidy, Gene Autry, Roy Rogers, and John Wayne?

6) Who received the only Oscar made of wood?

7) What is the name of Katharine Hepburn's character in *The African Queen*?

8) What boxer's life is depicted in *Raging Bull*?

9) What film won Rod Steiger a best actor Oscar?

10) What movie ends with the line "After all, tomorrow is another day"?

Quiz 37 Answers

1) Rin Tin Tin – The Academy wanted to appear more serious and have a human win, so they removed him from the ballot and voted again.

2) *It's a Mad, Mad, Mad, Mad World*

3) Barbra Streisand

4) Cutting the heads off parking meters

5) Gabby Hayes

6) Edgar Bergen and Charlie McCarthy

7) Rose Sayer

8) Jake LaMotta

9) *In the Heat of the Night*

10) *Gone with the Wind*

Quiz 38

1) Who are the only two people to win both a Nobel Prize and an Oscar?

2) Who appeared in more than 30 Alfred Hitchcock films?

3) Who has won the most best director Oscars?

4) What song does Rick ask Sam to play in *Casablanca*?

5) What is the name of Dustin Hoffman's character in *Midnight Cowboy*?

6) Who is the first character to speak in *Star Wars*?

7) Who wrote and directed *American Graffiti*?

8) Who played the tunnel king in *The Great Escape*?

9) In what country is John Wayne's *The Quiet Man* set?

10) What was the second movie to pair Richard Gere and Julia Roberts?

Quiz 38 Answers

1) **George Bernard Shaw and Bob Dylan**
2) Alfred Hitchcock
3) John Ford - four
4) "As Time Goes By"
5) Ratso Rizzo
6) C-3PO
7) George Lucas
8) Charles Bronson
9) Ireland
10) *Runaway Bride*

Quiz 39

1) What movie earned Clint Eastwood his first best director Oscar?

2) What is the name of the romantic comedy starring Katharine Hepburn and Spencer Tracy that is set in what is now the NBC headquarters at 30 Rockefeller Center?

3) What crime thriller was the Coen brothers' first movie in 1984?

4) What actor won his first Oscar for 1981's *Arthur* at the age of 77?

5) Who played the Wicked Witch of the West in *The Wizard of Oz*?

6) Who was the first Australian born actor to win an Oscar?

7) What was the last Clint Eastwood spaghetti western?

8) What is the name of Frances McDormand's character in *Fargo*?

9) Why are Academy Awards called Oscars?

10) Who are the only two people to win posthumous acting Oscars?

Quiz 39 Answers

1) *Unforgiven*
2) *Desk Set*

Movies

3) *Blood Simple*

4) Sir John Gielgud

5) Margaret Hamilton

6) Geoffrey Rush – *Shine* in 1996

7) *The Good, the Bad and the Ugly* – 1966

8) Marge Gunderson

9) Margaret Herrick, Academy librarian and future executive director, thought the statue looked like her uncle Oscar.

10) Peter Finch in 1976 for *Network* and Heath Ledger in 2008 for *The Dark Knight*

Science and Nature

Quiz 1

1) What is extracted from the ore cinnabar?
2) Who is the Bluetooth wireless technology named after?
3) What medical condition is detected using the Ishihara test?
4) What condition is singultus?
5) In computing, what is half of a byte called?
6) What sense is most closely linked to memory?
7) What are the only two elements that are liquid at room temperature?
8) What is the only rock that floats in water?
9) Hansen's disease is more commonly known as what?
10) What is the second hardest gem after diamond?

Quiz 1 Answers

1) Mercury
2) King Harald "Bluetooth" Gormsson – He ruled Denmark in the 10th century.
3) Color blindness
4) Hiccups
5) Nibble
6) Smell
7) Mercury and bromine
8) Pumice
9) Leprosy
10) Sapphire

Quiz 2

1) What scale is used to measure wind speed?
2) What planet is often called the Earth's twin because it is nearly the same size and mass and has similar composition?

3) A positive number that equals the sum of its divisors excluding itself is called what?

4) What is saffron made from?

5) What is the second largest planet in our solar system?

6) The heat of chili peppers is measured in what?

7) The density of what is measured on the Ringelmann Scale?

8) What two planets in our solar system don't have moons?

9) What is the lightest known solid element?

10) The Fields Medal is awarded for achievement in what field?

Quiz 2 Answers

1) Beaufort

2) Venus

3) Perfect number

4) Crocus flowers – Only the stigma part of the flower is used; it takes 70,000 to 250,000 flowers to make one pound of saffron.

5) Saturn

6) Scoville Heat Units

7) Smoke

8) Mercury and Venus

9) Lithium

10) Mathematics

Quiz 3

1) What number on the Richter scale does an earthquake have to reach to be considered major?

2) What scale is used to measure the hardness of minerals?

3) On what planet, other than Earth, did a man-made object first land?

4) What color has the longest wavelength in the visible spectrum?

5) Where in the human body is the labyrinth?

6) What is the largest nerve in the human body?

7) What does the human lacrimal gland produce?

8) The Fahrenheit and Celsius temperature scales are the same at

what temperature?

9) What device converts alternating current into direct current?

10) The small intestine is made up of the jejunum, ileum, and what?

Quiz 3 Answers

1) Seven
2) Mohs scale
3) Mars
4) Red
5) Ear
6) Sciatic
7) Tears
8) 40 degrees below zero
9) Rectifier
10) Duodenum

Quiz 4

1) Who invented carbonated soda water?
2) What is the male part of a flower called?
3) What are the four types of adult human teeth?
4) Where does Earth rank in size among the planets in our solar system?
5) Syncope is the medical name for what condition?
6) What element has the lowest boiling point?
7) What is the heaviest naturally occurring element?
8) Who invented the exploding shell?
9) During hot or dry periods, what is the equivalent of hibernation?
10) The process where food browns during cooking is known as what?

Quiz 4 Answers

1) Joseph Priestley – also discovered oxygen
2) Stamen
3) Incisors, canines, premolars, molars

4) Fifth

5) Fainting

6) Helium – negative 452.1 degrees Fahrenheit

7) Uranium

8) Henry Shrapnel

9) Estivation

10) Maillard reaction

Quiz 5

1) Where on the human body are the most sweat glands?

2) The chemical formula H_2O_2 refers to what?

3) What is the point in the Moon's orbit that is farthest from the Earth called?

4) After nitrogen and oxygen, what is the third most abundant gas in the atmosphere?

5) What species is the oldest living individual tree?

6) What metal is the best conductor of electricity?

7) Who discovered X-rays?

8) What is the only part of the human body that cannot repair itself?

9) Thomas Edison was involved in a rivalry over which form of electricity would be commercialized; Edison supported direct current; who was his rival that supported alternating current?

10) The Big Dipper is part of what constellation?

Quiz 5 Answers

1) Bottom of the feet

2) Hydrogen peroxide

3) Apogee

4) Argon

5) Bristlecone pine – 5,000 years

6) Silver – It is slightly more conductive than copper but much more expensive.

7) Wilhelm Roentgen

8) Teeth

9) Nikola Tesla

10) Ursa Major or Great Bear

Quiz 6

1) After calcium, what is the second most abundant mineral in the human body?

2) What are the Magellanic Clouds?

3) Lateral epicondylitis is the medical name for what common medical condition?

4) Who is the author of *Coming of Age in Samoa*, the mostly widely read book in the field of anthropology?

5) From what plant is the poison ricin obtained?

6) What is an apparatus that converts molecules into ions and separates the ions according to their mass-to-charge ratio called?

7) What is rayon made from?

8) On the periodic table, what is the first element alphabetically?

9) What does AM stand for on radios?

10) How much longer is a day on Mars than a day on Earth?

Quiz 6 Answers

1) Phosphorus

2) Galaxies

3) Tennis elbow

4) Margaret Mead

5) Castor oil plant

6) Mass spectrometer

7) Wood pulp

8) Actinium

9) Amplitude modulation

10) 40 minutes

Quiz 7

1) What is the most abundant element in the universe?

2) What is the opposite of nocturnal?

3) Stonehenge is made of what two main types of rock?

4) The Saffir-Simpson scale measures the intensity of what?

5) How long is an eon?

6) What is the name for the point in a planet's orbit when it is nearest the Sun?

7) What is the name of the process where plants lose water into the atmosphere?

8) What part of the human body is the axilla?

9) In the electromagnetic spectrum, what comes between X-rays and visible light?

10) What is the practice of concealing a file, message, image, or video within another file, message, image, or video called?

Quiz 7 Answers

1) Hydrogen – about 75% of the universe's mass

2) Diurnal

3) Bluestone and sandstone

4) Hurricanes

5) 1 billion years

6) Perihelion

7) Transpiration

8) Armpit

9) Ultraviolet light

10) Steganography

Quiz 8

1) What standard international unit of power is equal to 1.341 horsepower?

2) Where will you find the Malpighi's pyramids?

3) What is the number 10 to the power of 100 called?

4) What element is named after the Greek word for green?

5) What name is given to the socket in the human skull that holds the eye?

6) How many vertebrae in the human spine?

7) The atomic mass in the periodic table is stated relative to the weight of what element?

8) What is the standard international unit of force?

9) From what plant is the heart drug digitalis obtained?

10) The phenomenon where hot water may freeze faster than cold is known as what?

Quiz 8 Answers

1) Kilowatt

2) Kidneys – cone shaped tissues

3) Googol

4) Chlorine

5) Orbit

6) 33

7) Carbon – more specifically carbon-12

8) Newton – One newton equals the force needed to accelerate one kilogram of mass at the rate of one meter per second squared.

9) Foxglove

10) Mpemba Effect

Quiz 9

1) Most of the world's supply of cork comes from what type of tree?

2) Due to its unique chemical qualities, what natural food can remain in an edible form for centuries?

3) What is the smallest named time interval?

4) What is the effect of the Earth's rotation on the wind called?

5) What is the most abundant metal in the Earth's crust?

6) What name is given to a chemical reaction that takes in heat?

7) Who formulated the laws which first explained the movements of the planets properly?

8) What color is at the top of a rainbow?

9) What gives onions their distinctive smell?

10) What is the brightest star in the night sky?

Quiz 9 Answers

1) Oak – cork oak trees predominantly in Portugal and Spain
2) Honey – Three-thousand-year-old edible honey has been found in tombs.
3) Planck time – 5.39×10^{-44} seconds
4) Coriolis
5) Aluminum
6) Endothermic
7) Johannes Kepler
8) Red – Violet is at the bottom.
9) Sulfur – When cut or crushed, a chemical reaction changes an amino acid to a sulfur compound.
10) Sirius – Dog Star

Quiz 10

1) What planet in our solar system has the longest day?
2) What are metals not considered precious called?
3) What is the only planet in our solar system less dense than water?
4) An astronomical unit is defined by what distance?
5) Located near the root of human hair follicles, the arrector pili muscles are responsible for what phenomenon?
6) What figure has four sides all the same length but no right angles?
7) What was the name of the first electronic general-purpose computer?
8) What blood type qualifies as a universal donor?
9) What year was the first email sent?
10) What is the only tree that grows in saltwater?

Quiz 10 Answers

1) Venus – 243 Earth days
2) Base metals
3) Saturn
4) Earth to the Sun – 93 million miles

5) Goosebumps

6) Rhombus

7) ENIAC – 1946

8) O negative

9) 1971

10) Mangrove

Quiz 11

1) What are the four states of matter observable in everyday life?

2) What is the largest two-digit prime number?

3) Marble is formed by the metamorphosis of what rock?

4) What is the densest naturally occurring element?

5) In its natural form, aspirin comes from the bark of what tree?

6) What metal has the highest melting point?

7) How many times does the Moon revolve around the Earth in a year?

8) What is the smallest organ in the human body?

9) What is the largest 3-digit prime number?

10) The European organization for nuclear research is known by what four letters?

Quiz 11 Answers

1) Solid, liquid, gas, plasma

2) 97

3) Limestone

4) Osmium – about 25 times denser than water

5) White willow tree

6) Tungsten – 6,192 degrees Fahrenheit

7) 13

8) Pineal gland – in the center of the brain

9) 997

10) CERN – from the French "Conseil Europeen pour la Recherche Nucleaire"

Quiz 12

1) What is the study of fungi called?
2) Pascal is a measure of what?
3) What is the best-selling personal computer model of all time?
4) What is the longest muscle in the human body?
5) How many orbits has the Sun made around the center of the Milky Way Galaxy in its life?
6) Who first proposed the concept of contact lenses?
7) What planet in our solar system has the shortest day?
8) What is the equivalent megapixels of the human eye?
9) Approximately 2% of all people have what eye color?
10) How many constellations are in the night sky?

Quiz 12 Answers

1) Mycology
2) Pressure
3) Commodore 64 – 17 million units with a 1 MHz processor and 64KB RAM
4) Sartorius – from the pelvis to just below the inside of the knee
5) About 20
6) Leonardo da Vinci
7) Jupiter – 10 hours
8) 576 megapixels
9) Green – Brown is 55%; hazel and blue are 8% each.
10) 88

Quiz 13

1) What is the tallest mountain in the known universe?
2) What are the four lobes of the human brain?
3) How many planets in our solar system have moons?
4) What planet in our solar system has the most moons?
5) What is the densest planet in our solar system?
6) What is the most malleable naturally occurring metal?

7) What year was the first Apple computer released?

8) What human organ has the highest percentage of fat?

9) What is the only part of the human body without a blood supply?

10) What is the more common name for an Einstein Rosen Bridge?

Quiz 13 Answers

1) Olympus Mons on Mars – 69,459 feet

2) Frontal, occipital, parietal, temporal

3) Six – Earth, Mars, Jupiter, Saturn, Uranus, Neptune

4) Jupiter – 63

5) Earth

6) Gold

7) 1976

8) Brain – up to 60% fat

9) Cornea

10) Wormhole

Quiz 14

1) What year was the first cell phone call made?

2) What is the fastest healing part of the human body?

3) What two planets in our solar system rotate clockwise?

4) What is the name for the dark gray color the eyes see in perfect darkness because of optic nerve signals?

5) What is the smallest muscle in the human body?

6) How many bones do human babies have?

7) The first web site was launched by CERN in what year?

8) What is the hottest planet in our solar system?

9) What is the closest galaxy to our own Milky Way?

10) Where are the Islands of Langerhans?

Quiz 14 Answers

1) 1973

2) Tongue

3) Venus and Uranus

4) Eigengrau

5) Stapedius – in the middle ear

6) 300 – Some fuse together to form the 206 bones in adults.

7) 1991

8) Venus – 864 degrees Fahrenheit

9) Andromeda – 2.5 million light-years

10) Human pancreas – produce insulin

Quiz 15

1) In what year will Halley's Comet next appear?

2) If you hear thunder about 15 seconds after seeing lightning, how far away was the lightning?

3) What is the largest moon in our solar system?

4) What year was the first internet domain name registered?

5) In communications, what does VOIP stand for?

6) Sphenopalatine ganglioneuralgia is the medical term for what?

7) How many zeroes in a sextillion?

8) Who invented the electric battery in 1800?

9) In the human body, the hallux is more commonly known as what?

10) In 1997, what was the first mammal to be cloned from an adult cell?

Quiz 15 Answers

1) 2061 – last seen in 1986

2) About three miles - Sound travels about one mile in five seconds.

3) Ganymede – moon of Jupiter, about 41% of the size of Earth

4) 1985

5) Voice over internet protocol

6) Brain freeze – ice cream headache

7) 21

8) Alessandro Volta

9) Big toe

10) Dolly the sheep

Quiz 16

1) What is the name for a three-dimensional object that has only one surface and has no orientation?

2) What name is given to atoms with the same number of protons but different numbers of neutrons?

3) A sequence of numbers where each number is the sum of the two prior numbers is called what?

4) How long can a human live unprotected in space?

5) In space, what color would the Sun appear to be?

6) What was the first man made object in space?

7) Astronauts in space are trained to go to the bathroom every two hours; why?

8) While alone in the *Apollo 15* command module orbiting the Moon in 1971, astronaut Al Worden set what world record?

9) Why do Russian astronauts take guns into space?

10) Neil Armstrong didn't say, "That's one small step for man, one giant leap for mankind," when he set foot on the Moon; what did he say?

Quiz 16 Answers

1) Mobius strip – such as a strip of paper with a half twist joined at the ends

2) Isotopes

3) Fibonacci sequence

4) About 30 seconds – if they don't hold their breath

5) White

6) German V2 rocket – 1942

7) You can't tell if your bladder is full in space.

8) Most isolated human ever – He was 2,235 miles from the nearest human.

9) To protect themselves from bears if they land off course

10) "That's one small step for a man, one giant leap for mankind" – That is what Armstrong insisted he said; the word "a" before man wasn't heard clearly.

Quiz 17

1) What year was the word scientist first used?
2) What was the occupation of the first person to propose the big bang origin of the universe?
3) What planet in our solar system has a longer day than its year?
4) Who is the only person to win Nobel Prizes in two different areas of science?
5) What is the world's most visited website?
6) What is the first part of the human body to form in the womb?
7) What is the speed in miles per hour of the Earth's orbit around the Sun?
8) In 1991, the world's first webcam was created to do what?
9) How do the Moon and Sun fit together so perfectly in a solar eclipse?
10) Who first proposed that the Sun was the center around which the planets orbit?

Quiz 17 Answers

1) 1833
2) Priest – Georges Lemaitre
3) Venus – 243 days for one rotation (1 day), 225 days for one orbit around the Sun (1 year)
4) Marie Curie – physics and chemistry
5) Google
6) Asshole – Every human starts out as an asshole.
7) 66,600 mph
8) Check the status of a coffee pot at Cambridge University
9) By chance, the Sun is about 400 times larger than the Moon, and it is also about 400 times further away from the Earth, so the two appear to be the same size in the sky.
10) Aristarchus of Samos in the third century BC - Copernicus developed a fully predictive model in the 16th century but wasn't the first to propose the concept.

Quiz 18

1) What is a galactic or cosmic year?

2) The Catholic church made Galileo recant his theory that the Earth revolves around the Sun; how many years later did the church declare Galileo was right?

3) The most perfectly round natural object known in the universe is star 5,000 light-years away; prior to that discovery, what was the most perfectly round natural object known?

4) How many people do you need in a group to have a 50% chance that two will have the same birthday?

5) What does WIFI stand for?

6) What was the first item bought and sold across the internet in 1971?

7) What is the layer of the atmosphere closest to the Earth's surface called?

8) What is extirpation?

9) The human eye can differentiate more shades of what color than any other?

10) In the human body, what is a limbal dermoid?

Quiz 18 Answers

1) The amount of time it takes the Sun to orbit once around the center of the Milky Way Galaxy – about 225 million years

2) 359 years – in 1992

3) Sun

4) 23 – It is known as the Birthday Paradox; the probability goes up to 99.9% with just 70 people.

5) Nothing – It doesn't mean wireless fidelity or anything else; it is just a branding name picked by a company hired for the purpose.

6) Marijuana – Stanford students buying from MIT students.

7) Troposphere

8) Local extinction – Species is extinct locally but still exists elsewhere.

9) Green – That is why night vision goggles are green.

10) A cyst in the eye formed in the womb when skin cells get misplaced in the eye. The cyst can grow hair, cartilage, sweat glands, even

teeth just like skin can.

Quiz 19

1) Water doesn't conduct electricity well, so why is electricity so dangerous with water?
2) Walnuts, almonds, pecans, and cashews aren't technically nuts; what are they?
3) When you die, what sense is the last to go?
4) Apples, peaches, and raspberries belong to what plant family?
5) In total darkness, most people naturally adjust to how long of a cycle instead of 24 hours?
6) What parts of the human body never stop growing?
7) In terms of how long it takes to process input, what is the fastest human sense?
8) What planet has the strongest winds in our solar system?
9) On average, what is the coldest planet in our solar system?
10) Mohs hardness scale's hardest substance is diamond; what is the softest?

Quiz 19 Answers

1) The impurities in water make it a good conductor.
2) Drupes – also include peaches, plums and cherries. Drupes are a type of fruit where an outer fleshy part surrounds a shell or pit with a seed inside.
3) Hearing
4) Roses
5) 48 hours – 36 hours of activity and 12 hours of sleep
6) Ears and nose – parts composed of cartilage
7) Hearing – as little as 0.05 seconds
8) Neptune – more than 1,200 mph
9) Neptune – minus 353 degrees Fahrenheit
10) Talc

Quiz 20

1) What is the only bone in the human body that isn't attached to any

other bone?

2) What is mainly extracted from pitchblende?

3) Alphabetically, what is the last element in the periodic table?

4) Ageusia is the loss of what sense?

5) Who performed the first heart transplant?

6) What calculation device was invented by William Oughtred in 1662?

7) In 1971, what U.S. space probe was the first to orbit another planet?

8) The camellia sinensis evergreen shrub produces what?

9) What do you use your zygomaticus muscle for?

10) What is the white trail behind a jet plane comprised of?

Quiz 20 Answers

1) Hyoid bone – in the throat

2) Uranium

3) Zirconium

4) Taste

5) Dr. Christian Barnard

6) Slide rule

7) *Mariner 9*

8) Tea

9) Smiling

10) Ice crystals

Quiz 21

1) What is the world's tallest grass?

2) An alloy of iron, chromium, and nickel makes what?

3) What country grew the first orange?

4) What French philosopher created analytical geometry?

5) What are the world's smallest natural trees?

6) What is the most common infectious disease in the world?

7) Where on the human body is the thinnest skin?

8) The Easter lily is a native plant of what country?

9) Who first noticed that the Sun had spots?

10) In science, what can be up, down, strange, charm, top, or bottom?

Quiz 21 Answers

1) Bamboo
2) Stainless steel
3) China
4) Rene Descartes
5) Dwarf willows – They grow in Greenland and are only about two inches high.
6) Hepatitis B – More than one-quarter of the world's population is infected.
7) Eyelid - 0.05 mm thick. Palms and soles of feet are the thickest at 1.5 mm.
8) Japan
9) Galileo
10) quarks – types or flavors

Quiz 22

1) What drug was introduced by Bayer in 1898 and marketed as a non-addicting alternative to morphine and a treatment for cough inducing illnesses like bronchitis?
2) What compound puts the heat in chili peppers?
3) What is the hardest bone in the human body?
4) Who is known as the father of geometry?
5) What wheel did Blaise Pascal invent in search of perpetual motion?
6) Who established the science of genetics in 1866?
7) How many prime numbers are there that are less than 20?
8) How long does it take the Moon to revolve around the Earth to the nearest day?
9) What are the four major human blood types?
10) What is the common name for the fruit Citrus grandis?

Quiz 22 Answers

1) Heroin - The AMA approved it for general use in 1906 and recommended it as a morphine replacement; soon, there were

200,000 heroin addicts in New York City alone.

2) Capsaicin

3) Jawbone

4) Euclid

5) Roulette wheel

6) Gregor Mendel

7) Eight numbers – 2, 3, 5, 7, 11, 13, 17, 19

8) 27 days

9) A, B, AB, O

10) Grapefruit

Quiz 23

1) Atoms stop moving at what temperature?

2) What Polish astronomer demonstrated in 1512 that the Sun is the center of the solar system?

3) What is the largest gland in the human body?

4) What five tastes can a human distinguish?

5) What is a googolplexian?

6) What planet in our solar system has the shortest year?

7) What is the end cause of every human death?

8) What is the fastest growing plant?

9) What month is the Earth closest to the Sun?

10) The word laser is an acronym for what?

Quiz 23 Answers

1) Zero degrees Kelvin or absolute zero – equivalent to minus 459.67 degrees Fahrenheit

2) Nicholas Copernicus

3) Liver

4) Sweet, sour, bitter, salty, umami

5) The largest named number – A googol is 1 followed by 100 zeroes; a googolplex is 1 followed by a googol of zeroes; a googolplexian is 1 followed by a googolplex of zeroes.

6) Mercury – 88 Earth days

7) Cerebral hypoxia – Lack of oxygen to the brain is the final cause of death regardless what initiates it.

8) Bamboo – Some species can grow three feet in a day.

9) January

10) Light amplification by stimulated emission of radiation

Quiz 24

1) What is the largest muscle in the human body?
2) What is the longest bone in the human body?
3) What is the simplest gem in chemical composition?
4) Who discovered Saturn's rings?
5) What part of the eye continues to grow throughout a person's life?
6) What is the most frequently broken bone in the human body?
7) What are the three major classifications for rocks?
8) What plant does natural vanilla flavoring come from?
9) What tiny vessel connects an artery with a vein?
10) In math, what does a "lemniscate" shape mean?

Quiz 24 Answers

1) Gluteus maximus
2) Femur
3) Diamond – composed only of carbon
4) Galileo
5) Lens
6) Clavicle or collar bone
7) Igneous, metamorphic, sedimentary
8) Orchid
9) Capillary
10) Infinity - Lemniscate is a shape with two loops meeting at a central point.

Quiz 25

1) What is the oldest known vegetable?
2) What is the clotting protein in blood called?

3) What metal is the major constituent of rubies?

4) What is the hardest substance in the human body?

5) What do astronomers call a giant cloud of gas and dust?

6) About 2,400 years ago, what did Hippocrates describe as "man's best medicine"?

7) What is the process of wave like muscle contractions that moves food in the digestive tract starting in the esophagus called?

8) What was the first man-made object to leave the solar system?

9) Which isotope of carbon is used for radiocarbon dating?

10) What is the first prime number after 1,000,000?

Quiz 25 Answers

1) Pea

2) Fibrin

3) Aluminum

4) Tooth enamel

5) Nebula

6) Walking

7) Peristalsis

8) *Pioneer 10*

9) Carbon-14

10) 1,000,003

Quiz 26

1) What was the very first animal to go into space?

2) Who is the oldest person ever to go into space?

3) What planet circles the Sun every 84 years?

4) Who was the first person to explain why the sky is blue?

5) What is the only country in the world to have a net gain of trees in the last hundred years?

6) The average lightning bolt is about five miles long and how wide?

7) The busiest muscles in the human body are found where?

8) What color are sunsets on Mars?

9) What makes Mars red?

10) What country has the largest permanent scale model of the solar system?

Quiz 26 Answers

1) Fruit flies – They were sent up in 1947 in a captured V2 rocket and were recovered alive.

2) John Glenn – 77

3) Uranus

4) Leonardo da Vinci

5) Israel

6) One inch

7) Eyes – They move 100,000 times a day.

8) Blue

9) It is covered in iron oxide (rust).

10) Sweden – The Sun is represented by the largest hemispherical building in the world in Stockholm; the model is on a 1:20 million-scale and stretches for 950 kilometers.

Sports

Quiz 1

1) Who was the first woman to swim the English Channel?
2) How many disciplines are there in men's gymnastics?
3) Who has won the most heavyweight boxing title fights in history?
4) Who is the only starting pitcher in a World Series game to bat other than ninth?
5) What do Indianapolis 500 winners traditionally drink in the winner's circle?
6) What sport features a series of bouts known as a barrage?
7) Who was *Sports Illustrated's* first female sportsperson of the year?
8) How many players are there on a water polo team?
9) How many furlongs are there in a mile?
10) Famous pediatrician and author Benjamin Spock won an Olympic gold medal in what sport?

Quiz 1 Answers

1) Gertrude Ederle – 1926
2) Six - vault, rings, floor, high bar, parallel bars, horse
3) Joe Louis
4) Babe Ruth
5) Milk
6) Fencing
7) Billie Jean King - 1972
8) Seven
9) Eight
10) Rowing

Quiz 2

1) What was Mildred Didrikson Zaharias's nickname?
2) What title has been won by the rider who wears the polka dot jersey in the Tour de France?

3) Who was the first unseeded man to win Wimbledon?

4) Who was the last amateur tennis player to win the U.S. Open?

5) Cathy Rigby was the first woman to do what for *Sports Illustrated*?

6) Who is credited with inventing basketball?

7) What former Olympian lit the flame at the 1996 Atlanta Olympic games?

8) Who is the only Major League Baseball player to win MVP in both leagues?

9) Who is Edson Arantes do Nascimento better known as?

10) What sport are Torvill and Dean famous for?

Quiz 2 Answers

1) Babe – one of the greatest female athletes of all time

2) King of the Mountains

3) Boris Becker - 1985

4) Arthur Ashe – 1968

5) Pose nude

6) James Naismith

7) Muhammad Ali

8) Frank Robinson

9) Pele – Brazilian soccer player

10) Ice dancing

Quiz 3

1) The coldest NFL game in history was played where?

2) Who was the first tennis player to achieve the calendar year grand slam?

3) Who was the first thoroughbred horse to win 1 million dollars?

4) Over what distance is a human steeplechase run?

5) Who is the youngest man to win the Wimbledon tennis singles title?

6) Who is the only person to ever play in the Super Bowl and World Series?

7) What is the longest track and field race in the Olympics?

8) What is the first event in the decathlon?

9) What university originated the football huddle?

10) What sport is played 11 on a side on ice with a ball?

Quiz 3 Answers

1) Green Bay – 1967 NFL championship

2) Don Budge – 1938

3) Citation – last Triple Crown winner prior to Secretariat

4) 3,000 meters

5) Boris Becker – 17

6) Deion Sanders

7) 50-kilometer walking race

8) 100 meters

9) Gallaudet University (school for the deaf) in 1892 - They huddled to avoid the other team seeing their sign language.

10) Bandy

Quiz 4

1) In a game of horseshoes, how many feet apart are the stakes?

2) What piece of sporting equipment has a maximum length of 42 inches and a maximum diameter of 2.61 inches?

3) Mintonette was the original name of what sport?

4) What is the fastest racquet sport?

5) What sport is played on the largest field?

6) What sports hero wore a cabbage leaf under his cap?

7) In cricket, how many runs are scored if the ball is hit over the boundary without bouncing?

8) What is the only sport where you can see teams defending goals of different sizes?

9) What outdoor game is won by "pegging out"?

10) Who was the first African American after Arthur Ashe to win a Wimbledon singles title?

Quiz 4 Answers

1) 40 feet
2) Baseball bat
3) Volleyball
4) Badminton – The shuttlecock can travel over 200 mph.
5) Polo – 300 yards by 160 yards
6) Babe Ruth – He put chilled cabbage leaves under his cap to keep cool.
7) Six
8) Water polo – The goal at the deep end is smaller than the goal at the shallow end.
9) Croquet
10) Venus Williams

Quiz 5

1) Who was the second person to run a sub four-minute mile?
2) In what year did Eddie the Eagle Edwards leap to stardom at the winter Olympics?
3) In which Olympics did Mark Spitz win seven gold medals?
4) Singer Johnny Mathis was a world class athlete in what event?
5) The Emperors Cup is awarded in what sport?
6) What was the first U.S. hockey team to win the Stanley Cup?
7) Where is the world's largest bullfighting ring?
8) Who became the oldest rookie in Major League Baseball at age 42?
9) What Wimbledon singles champion had a part in a John Wayne film?
10) Who was the first Major League Baseball player to strike out 4,000 batters?

Quiz 5 Answers

1) John Landy
2) 1988
3) 1972 – Munich
4) High jump – He was invited to the Olympic trials when he got a

recording contract; his major high jump competitor in the San Francisco Bay area where he grew up was future NBA Hall of Fame star Bill Russell.

5) Sumo wrestling

6) Seattle Metropolitans in 1917 - The next season the National Hockey Association was replaced by the NHL; the Stanley Cup was first awarded in 1893.

7) Mexico City

8) Satchel Paige

9) Althea Gibson - *The Horse Soldiers*

10) Nolan Ryan

Quiz 6

1) What was the last country to host both the summer and the winter Olympic games in the same year?

2) How many throwing events are there in a decathlon?

3) Who is the oldest Olympic swimmer to win a medal?

4) What is the only sports team to play on all seven continents?

5) Who is the only person to win the tennis grand slam (win all four grand slam tournaments in a calendar year) twice?

6) What sport takes place in a 4.55-meter diameter circle?

7) What single sporting event has the most in person spectators in the world?

8) How many stitches are on a regulation baseball?

9) The Greek god Apollo accidentally killed his friend Hyacinthus while practicing what sporting event?

10) In what year did the last Major League Baseball player bat .400?

Quiz 6 Answers

1) Germany – 1936

2) Three – discus, shot put, javelin

3) Dara Torres – 41

4) Harlem Globetrotters

5) Rod Laver

6) Sumo wrestling

7) Tour de France bicycle race - 12 to 15 million
8) 108
9) Discus
10) 1941 – Ted Williams

Quiz 7

1) Who was *Sports Illustrated's* first Sportsman of the Year in 1954?
2) How much does a U.S. athlete get for winning an Olympic gold medal?
3) What year were the first Winter Olympics held?
4) What year was the first Kentucky Derby run?
5) How many golf major championships did Jack Nicklaus win?
6) What two Major League Baseball teams share the record for most wins in a season at 116?
7) Where did curling originate?
8) What four horses have won the Triple Crown since Secretariat in 1973?
9) In what country did table tennis originate?
10) How many feet wide is a regulation NFL football field?

Quiz 7 Answers

1) Roger Bannister – first sub four-minute mile
2) $25,000
3) 1924
4) 1875
5) 18
6) Chicago Cubs (1906 in a 154-game season) and Seattle Mariners (2001 in a 162-game season)
7) Scotland
8) Seattle Slew, Affirmed, American Pharoah, Justify
9) England – late 19th century
10) 160

Quiz 8

1) Who is the only NBA player to score 100 points in a game?
2) Horse racing's Triple Crown has only been won once in consecutive years; what years?
3) What country has won the most Winter Olympics medals?
4) Who was the last Major League Baseball pitcher to win 30 or more games in a season?
5) What was Babe Ruth's first name?
6) What NFL team was originally called the Senors?
7) How many players are on the field at one time in a men's lacrosse game?
8) How many times have the Olympics been canceled?
9) What is the oldest championship in North American professional sports?
10) Who is the youngest woman to ever win a tennis grand slam singles title?

Quiz 8 Answers

1) Wilt Chamberlain
2) 1977 and 1978 – Seattle Slew and Affirmed
3) Norway
4) Denny McLain – 1968
5) George
6) Oakland Raiders – The original name was winner of a name the team contest; it was changed to Raiders, the third-place name, after nine days.
7) 20
8) Three – 1916, 1940, 1944
9) Stanley Cup – 1893
10) Martina Hingis – 16 years 3 months

Quiz 9

1) What year were the first modern Olympics held?
2) Who has appeared on the most *Sports Illustrated* covers?

3) In what sport is the Iroquois Cup awarded?

4) Who is the only golfer to complete a calendar year Grand Slam?

5) How many U.S. cities have hosted the Summer Olympics?

6) Who holds the Major League Baseball record for career strikeouts as a batter?

7) What year did the last undefeated team win the Super Bowl?

8) How many feet long is a regulation NBA basketball court?

9) What country has won the most soccer World Cups?

10) What is the largest population city in the U.S. that doesn't have an MLB, NFL, NBA, or NHL team?

Quiz 9 Answers

1) 1896 – Athens

2) Michael Jordan

3) Lacrosse

4) Bobby Jones – 1930

5) Three – St. Louis (1904), Los Angeles (1932, 1984), and Atlanta (1996)

6) Reggie Jackson

7) 1972 - Miami

8) 94 feet

9) Brazil

10) Austin, Texas – 11th largest city in U.S.

Quiz 10

1) How many feet wide is a regulation volleyball court?

2) How many Olympic games have been hosted in Africa?

3) Who was the first American to win the Tour de France bicycle race?

4) What U.S. city was first to host the Olympics?

5) Who holds the NBA record for most career fouls?

6) Who was the first athlete on a Wheaties box?

7) Who was the first American to win the Olympic marathon gold medal?

8) What is the last event in the decathlon?

9) What hockey player has won the most Stanley Cups?

10) What year was the first Indianapolis 500 race?

Quiz 10 Answers

1) 30 feet

2) Zero

3) Greg Lemond – 1986

4) St. Louis – 1904

5) Kareem Abdul-Jabbar

6) Lou Gehrig

7) Frank Shorter – 1972

8) 1500 meters

9) Henri Richard – 11 with the Montreal Canadiens

10) 1911

Quiz 11

1) What year did China make its first appearance in the Summer Olympics?

2) Who is the youngest player inducted to the Hockey Hall of Fame?

3) Of all the players in North American men's professional sports, who has won the most MVP awards?

4) How many games long was Joe DiMaggio's MLB consecutive hit streak record?

5) Who is the only NBA player to win MVP, defensive player of the year, and finals MVP in the same year?

6) According to NBA rules, how long does a player have to shoot a free throw after catching the ball?

7) In what country was the famous Rumble in the Jungle boxing match between Muhammad Ali and George Foreman fought?

8) Who is the only world heavyweight boxing champion to finish his career undefeated?

9) Based on participants, soccer is the most popular sport in the world; what is the second most popular sport?

10) Based on global following, soccer is the most popular sport in the world, what is the second most popular?

Quiz 11 Answers

1) 1984
2) Bobby Orr – 31
3) Wayne Gretzky – nine
4) 56
5) Hakeem Olajuwon
6) 10 seconds
7) Zaire
8) Rocky Marciano
9) Badminton – followed by field hockey
10) Cricket – followed by field hockey

Quiz 12

1) Who is the youngest ever world heavyweight boxing champion?
2) What were the first two women's sports included in the modern Olympics?
3) Who was the first Olympic boxing gold medalist to also win a boxing world championship?
4) What was the first U.S. college sport to name an All-American team?
5) In 1457, King James II of Scotland banned what two sports because they interfered with archery practice needed for national defense?
6) In horse racing, which of the Triple Crown races is the shortest?
7) At the ancient Olympic games, what did they use as archery targets?
8) In what sport did the word stymie originate?
9) What is the only country to have won medals in the Winter Olympics but never in the Summer Olympics?
10) Who is the only person to win the Heisman Trophy twice?

Quiz 12 Answers

1) Mike Tyson – 20
2) Tennis and golf - 1900
3) Floyd Patterson – 1952 Olympics and 1956 world champion

4) Football – 1889

5) Golf and soccer

6) Preakness – 1 3/16 miles

7) Tethered doves

8) Golf – Until 1952 when the rules were changed, balls had to remain in place, so you could be stymied by having another player's ball between your ball and the hole; you had to loft your ball over the other ball.

9) Liechtenstein

10) Archie Griffin – Ohio State in 1974 and 1975

Quiz 13

1) Who pitched the only no-hit game in World Series history?

2) In golf, what do you call a score of four under par on a single hole?

3) Who is the only coach to win both an NCAA Division I basketball championship and an NBA title?

4) What is the only U.S. city to win three of the four major professional sports championships in the same year?

5) Who won the most consecutive Wimbledon singles titles?

6) Who holds the record for most consecutive PGA tour wins?

7) What pitcher holds the Major League Baseball record for most no hitters?

8) What athlete has appeared on the Wheaties box the most?

9) Who was the first non-American golfer to win the Masters?

10) How many feet wide is a regulation NBA court?

Quiz 13 Answers

1) Don Larsen – 1956

2) Condor – There have only been four verified; all were hole in ones on par five holes.

3) Larry Brown – Kansas in 1988 and Detroit Pistons in 2004

4) Detroit – 1935, won NFL, NBA, and NHL

5) Martina Navratilova – six

6) Byron Nelson – 11 in 1945

7) Nolan Ryan – seven

8) Michael Jordan

9) Gary Player – 1961

10) 50 feet

Quiz 14

1) In inches, how tall are the hurdles in a men's 110-meter hurdle race?

2) Only three people have won individual gold medals in the same event in four consecutive Olympics, who are they?

3) What is the length of a tennis court in feet?

4) What sport was transferred from the Summer Olympics to the Winter Olympics in 1924?

5) What is the first city to host the Summer Olympics three times?

6) What famous American statesman earned an honorary induction into the International Swimming Hall of Fame?

7) Why did the Russian Olympic team arrive 12 days late for the 1908 London Olympics?

8) Who is the only person to be number one in the world in both table tennis and tennis?

9) What year was the first NFL game televised?

10) What horse has the most Grand National Steeplechase wins?

Quiz 14 Answers

1) 42 inches

2) Michael Phelps (swimming 200-meter individual medley), Carl Lewis (long jump), Al Oerter (discus)

3) 78 feet

4) Ice hockey

5) London – 1908, 1948, 2012

6) Benjamin Franklin – He had a lifelong love of swimming and was an ardent proponent of it and invented some swim fins.

7) Russia was still using the Julian calendar instead of Gregorian.

8) Fred Perry – He won the 1929 world championship in table tennis and was the first player in tennis to win a career grand slam including three straight Wimbledon titles from 1934-1936.

9) 1939

10) Red Rum – three

Quiz 15

1) Giacomo Agostini won 122 Grand Prix and 15 world titles in what sport?

2) What were table tennis balls originally made from?

3) Barring rain, what is the only track & field event where you get wet?

4) In what sport are you banned from playing left handed?

5) What husband and wife both won gold medals at the 1952 Helsinki Summer Olympics?

6) Who was the first gymnast to score a perfect 10 in the Olympics?

7) In golf, what device is used to measure the speed of the greens?

8) What horse has the fastest times ever for the Kentucky Derby, Preakness, and Belmont?

9) Who broke the world record over 30 times in the pole vault?

10) What nine-time Olympic champion was known as the Flying Finn?

Quiz 15 Answers

1) Motorcycle racing

2) Cork – from wine bottles

3) Steeplechase

4) Polo - If a left-handed and right-handed player went for the ball, they would collide.

5) Emil and Dana Zatopek - Emil won the 5,000 meters, 10,000 meters, and marathon (he had never run a marathon before); Dana won the javelin.

6) Nadia Comaneci

7) Stimpmeter

8) Secretariat

9) Sergey Bubka

10) Paavo Nurmi

Quiz 16

1) Who is the only coach to win both an NBA and WNBA title?
2) What is the oldest stroke in competitive swimming?
3) What city hosted the first winter Olympics in Asia?
4) What is the world's oldest golf course?
5) What is the highest elevation city to host the Summer Olympics?
6) What year did Roger Maris hit 61 home runs?
7) What is the only host country not to win a gold medal at its own summer Olympics?
8) **Who was the first U.S. high school athlete to run a mile in under four minutes?**
9) For racing purposes, what is the birthday of all horses in the Northern Hemisphere?
10) How high is a soccer goal?

Quiz 16 Answers

1) Paul Westhead – Los Angeles Lakers and Phoenix Mercury
2) Breaststroke
3) Sapporo, Japan - 1972
4) St. Andrews, Scotland
5) Mexico City
6) 1961
7) Canada – Montreal Olympics in 1976
8) Jim Ryun
9) January 1 – A horse born on December 31 is one year old on January 1.
10) Eight feet

Quiz 17

1) What is the theme song of the Harlem Globetrotters?
2) In what sport does a player use a cesta to hurl a pelota?
3) What two cities usually mark the end points of English Channel swims?
4) How many horses are there on a polo team?

5) What is the straightaway opposite the one with the finish line in horse racing called?

6) What is the captain of a curling team called?

7) What race was increased by 385 yards, so Edward VII could see the finish line better?

8) How many points is a ringer worth in horseshoes?

9) **What U.S. city has hosted two winter Olympics?**

10) How many cities have hosted the Olympics more than once?

Quiz 17 Answers

1) Sweet Georgia Brown

2) Jai-alai player

3) Calais and Dover

4) Four

5) Backstretch

6) Skip

7) Marathon at the 1908 London Olympics - 26 miles 385 yards became the standard distance thereafter.

8) Three

9) **Lake Placid – 1932 and 1980**

10) Seven – Athens, London, Paris, St. Moritz, Lake Placid, Los Angeles, Innsbruck

Quiz 18

1) What is the most common team name for U.S. college football teams?

2) Who was the only female athlete at the 1976 summer Olympics not given a sex test?

3) How many players are there on a cricket side?

4) What year was the first Super Bowl played?

5) In darts, what is the highest score possible with three darts?

6) **What American speed skater won five gold medals at the 1980 winter Olympics?**

7) Who was forced to return his Olympic medals after it was learned he had played semi-pro baseball?

8) What sport features the fastest moving ball?

9) What is the diameter of a golf hole?

10) How wide is the home plate in baseball?

Quiz 18 Answers

1) Eagles

2) Princess Anne

3) 11

4) 1967

5) 180 – 3 triple 20s

6) **Eric Heiden**

7) Jim Thorpe

8) Jai-alai – up to 188 mph

9) 4 ¼ inches

10) 17 inches

Quiz 19

1) Who first flopped to win the 1968 Olympic high jump gold medal?

2) What woman won the only gold medal for the U.S. at the 1968 winter Olympics?

3) What is the Olympic motto?

4) What did Abebe Bikila go without in winning the 1960 Olympic marathon?

5) What are the two categories of harness racing?

6) How many seconds must a cowboy stay aboard a rodeo bronc?

7) What is the only community owned franchise in the NFL?

8) What movie Tarzan won the 400-meter freestyle swim in the 1932 Olympics?

9) What team has won the most NBA championships?

10) Who was the first African American to win the Wimbledon men's singles tennis title?

Quiz 19 Answers

1) Dick Fosbury – He invented the Fosbury flop which is now the

standard for high jumpers.

2) Peggy Fleming

3) Faster, higher, stronger or citius, altius, fortius in Latin

4) Shoes – He ran barefoot.

5) Trotting and pacing

6) Eight

7) Green Bay Packers

8) Buster Crabbe

9) Boston Celtics

10) Arthur Ashe

Quiz 20

1) How many Major League Baseball teams are named for birds?

2) Who was disqualified for performance enhancing drugs after winning the men's 100 meters at the 1988 Olympic games?

3) What year did the last undefeated team win the NCAA Division I basketball championship?

4) Who held seven American track records from 2,000 to 10,000 meters when he died in a 1975 car crash?

5) What famous U.S. general placed fifth in the pentathlon at the 1912 Olympics?

6) What actor finished runner-up in the Le Mans 24-hour auto race?

7) What are the three weapons used in fencing?

8) The Borg-Warner trophy is awarded for winning what?

9) Who is the only wild card entrant to win Wimbledon?

10) What is the only country that has played in every soccer World Cup tournament?

Quiz 20 Answers

1) Three – Cardinals, Orioles, Blue Jays

2) Ben Johnson

3) 1976 - Indiana

4) Steve Prefontaine

5) George S. Patton

6) Paul Newman
7) Epee, foil, saber
8) Indianapolis 500
9) Goran Ivanišević – 2001
10) Brazil

Television

Quiz 1

1) In the sitcom *Married with Children*, what is the dog's name?
2) The Daleks from *Doctor Who* come from what planet?
3) In *Star Trek*, what is the name of Spock's father?
4) What is the name of the train on *Petticoat Junction*?
5) What famous bird first appeared on television in September 1957?
6) What is the name of the family featured in *Father Knows Best*?
7) Bamboo Harvester was the real name of the actor who played what character?
8) What was the first animated series to run in U.S. prime time?
9) What are the character first names of the original *Charlie's Angels*?
10) What is the name of the company that the *Taxi* characters work for?

Quiz 1 Answers

1) Buck
2) Skaro
3) Sarek
4) Cannonball
5) NBC peacock
6) Anderson
7) Mr. Ed
8) *The Flintstones* – 1960
9) Sabrina, Kelly, Jill
10) Sunshine Cab

Quiz 2

1) What was the Lone Ranger's real name?
2) What show featured the first interracial kiss broadcast in the U.S.?
3) On *The X-Files*, what is Mulder's nickname?
4) What is the name of George of the Jungle's pet elephant?

5) Who lives at 0001 Cemetery Lane?

6) What is Batman's butler Alfred's last name?

7) What is the name of Dudley Do-Right's horse?

8) What actress played Emma Peel in *The Avengers*?

9) What planet is the space alien Alf from?

10) What 1980s sitcom featured Tom Hanks in drag?

Quiz 2 Answers

1) John Reid

2) *Star Trek*

3) Spooky

4) Shep

5) *Addams Family*

6) Pennyworth

7) Horse

8) Diana Rigg

9) Melmac

10) *Bosom Buddies*

Quiz 3

1) On *Leave It to Beaver*, what is Wally's best friend's name?

2) At the end of *M*A*S*H*, what character stayed in Korea?

3) Who became a genius whenever he put on the fabulous Kerwood Derby?

4) What cartoon character's catchphrase is "Exit, stage left!"?

5) What character did Patrick Macnee portray in *The Avengers*?

6) What is the name of Mulder and Scully's supervisor on *The X-Files*?

7) Who played Dr. McCoy in the original *Star Trek* series?

8) The Great Gazoo is an alien in what cartoon series?

9) What century is the setting for *Star Trek*?

10) Where did Rocky and Bullwinkle play college football?

Quiz 3 Answers

1) Eddie Haskell
2) Maxwell Klinger
3) Bullwinkle Moose
4) Snagglepuss
5) Jonathan Steed
6) Walter Skinner
7) DeForest Kelley
8) *The Flintstones*
9) 23rd century
10) Wossamotta U

Quiz 4

1) Who provided the voices of Bugs Bunny, Sylvester, and Tweety Pie?
2) Wile E. Coyote gets all his traps to try to catch the Roadrunner from what company?
3) What show has the catchphrase "And now for something completely different"?
4) Who played detective Frank Cannon?
5) On *The Beverly Hillbillies*, what is the name of the bank manager?
6) What was the first 90-minute U.S. series in 1962?
7) What sitcom character liked to eat cats?
8) What cartoon character's vital statistics are 19-19-19?
9) *Glee* is set at what high school?
10) On *Kung Fu*, what is Master Po's name for young Cain?

Quiz 4 Answers

1) Mel Blanc
2) Acme
3) *Monty Python's Flying Circus*
4) William Conrad
5) Milburn Drysdale
6) *The Virginian*

7) Alf
8) Olive Oyl
9) William McKinley
10) Grasshopper

Quiz 5

1) What cartoon character was originally called Egghead?
2) What is the name of Barbara Stanwyck's character on *The Big Valley*?
3) In 1994, what show broke ground depicting a gay marriage between innkeepers Ron and Erick?
4) What is the name of the ranger who is always after Yogi Bear?
5) What is the last name of the family in *Lost in Space*?
6) What prop was used as Dr. McCoy's medical scanner in *Star Trek*?
7) On *The Flintstones*, what fraternal order do Fred and Barney belong to?
8) What is Lucy's maiden name on *I Love Lucy*?
9) The maiden names of what two cartoon characters are Slaghoople and McBricker?
10) Charles Boyer inspired what cartoon character?

Quiz 5 Answers

1) Elmer Fudd
2) Victoria Barkley
3) *Northern Exposure*
4) Ranger Smith
5) Robinson
6) Salt shaker
7) Water Buffaloes
8) McGillicuddy
9) Wilma Flintstone and Betty Rubble
10) Pepe le Pew

Quiz 6

1) What character did Hank Ketcham create?
2) *Mork and Mindy* was a spin-off from what sitcom?
3) What children's show had the cartoon *Tom Terrific with Mighty Manfred the Wonder Dog*?
4) What actress played the barmaid Carla on *Cheers*?
5) Who were David Soul and Paul Michael Glaser better known as?
6) Who was the first celebrity to make a guest appearance on *Sesame Street*?
7) On *Mr. Ed*, what is Ed's owner's full name?
8) Who is the fastest mouse in all of Mexico?
9) Victor Buono played what villain in the original *Batman* series?
10) What star's baby appeared on the first cover of *TV Guide*?

Quiz 6 Answers

1) Dennis the Menace
2) *Happy Days*
3) *Captain Kangaroo*
4) Rhea Perlman
5) *Starsky and Hutch*
6) James Earl Jones – He appeared on the show's second episode.
7) Wilbur Post
8) Speedy Gonzalez
9) King Tut
10) Lucille Ball

Quiz 7

1) Who played Superman in the original series?
2) The theme music for *Monty Python's Flying Circus* was written by what composer?
3) Bugs Bunny often finds himself at the wrong end of a gun usually toted by what two characters?
4) Before starring in *Modern Family*, Ed O'Neill was best known for playing what television dad?

5) On *The Flintstones*, Dino is Fred's pet; what is Barney's pet called?
6) What cartoon character was born in a warren under the Brooklyn Dodgers' stadium?
7) Where does George Jetson work?
8) Who is Dick Dastardly's pet?
9) On *Frazier*, what is the dad's dog's name?
10) Who was the first *Saturday Night Live* cast member to also have their child become a cast member?

Quiz 7 Answers

1) George Reeves
2) John Philip Sousa – "The Liberty Bell March"
3) Elmer Fudd and Yosemite Sam
4) Al Bundy – *Married with Children*
5) Hoppy - a hoparoo
6) Bugs Bunny
7) Spacely Sprockets
8) Muttley
9) Eddie
10) Chris Elliot

Quiz 8

1) What is the Cookie Monster's real name on *Sesame Street*?
2) What U.S. show featured the first openly gay character?
3) What year did *American Bandstand* debut?
4) What was the first series filmed before a live audience?
5) What was the first toy advertised on U.S. television?
6) In what city does SpongeBob SquarePants live?
7) Who was the original host of *The Tonight Show*?
8) Besides his moose strength, what is Bullwinkle's great talent?
9) On what sitcom did Frank Sinatra make his final television appearance?
10) Who was the original host of *Jeopardy!*?

Quiz 8 Answers

1) Sid
2) *Soap* – 1977
3) 1952
4) *I Love Lucy*
5) Mr. Potato Head – 1952
6) Bikini Bottom
7) Steve Allen
8) He could remember everything he ever ate.
9) *Who's the Boss*
10) Art Fleming – 1964 to 1984

Quiz 9

1) What year did *Saturday Night Live* debut?
2) On *Star Trek*, what is Captain Kirk's middle name?
3) In what year is *Lost in Space* set?
4) What are the names of the two characters that heckle the rest of the cast from the balcony on *The Muppet Show*?
5) How many series were spun off from *All in the Family*?
6) What is the name of George Peppard's character on *The A Team*?
7) *The Simpsons* first debuted as a short on what show?
8) What character's real name is Gordon Shumway?
9) On *Seinfeld*, what is Kramer's first name?
10) What long running science fiction show first aired in November 1963?

Quiz 9 Answers

1) 1975
2) Tiberius
3) 1997
4) Statler and Waldorf
5) Seven – *Maude, Good Times, The Jeffersons, Checking In, Archie Bunker's Place, Gloria, 704 Hauser*

6) Hannibal Smith
7) *The Tracey Ullman Show*
8) Alf
9) Cosmo
10) *Doctor Who*

Quiz 10

1) What was the first U.S. network show without a theme song?
2) What U.S. show had the first toilet heard flushing?
3) Who was the youngest cast member ever of *Saturday Night Live*?
4) Who played the title role in the 1960s cult classic *The Prisoner*?
5) Who was Johnny Carson's final guest on *The Tonight Show*?
6) What year did *Sesame Street* debut?
7) What is the first name of the son on *Sanford and Son*?
8) What is Archie Bunker's son-in-law's full name on *All in the Family*?
9) What is the longest running scripted prime time show of all time?
10) What is the name of the son on *The Jetsons*?

Quiz 10 Answers

1) *60 Minutes*
2) *All in the Family* – 1971
3) Anthony Michael Hall – 17
4) Patrick McGoohan
5) Bette Midler
6) 1969
7) Lamont
8) Michael Stivic
9) *The Simpsons*
10) Elroy

Quiz 11

1) Who is the oldest person to host *Saturday Night Live*?

2) What was the most watched U.S. series finale of all time?

3) How tall is Big Bird on *Sesame Street*?

4) The character of Sheriff Andy Taylor first appeared on what show?

5) Who is Alex's youngest sibling on *Family Ties*?

6) What was the first U.S. network show to use the "F" word?

7) What was the first U.S. R-rated show?

8) What is the name of Norm's wife on *Cheers*?

9) What is the name of the inn on *Newhart*?

10) What is the name of the car on *Knight Rider*?

Quiz 11 Answers

1) Betty White – 88

2) *M*A*S*H*

3) 8 feet 2 inches

4) *The Danny Thomas Show* – later spun off to *The Andy Griffith Show*

5) Andy – He was born during the series run.

6) *Saturday Night Live*

7) *NYPD Blue* – 1993

8) Vera

9) Stratford Inn

10) Kitt – Knight Industries Two Thousand

Quiz 12

1) *Game of Thrones* is based on a series of novels by what author?

2) On the U.S. series *The Office*, what is the name of the company they work for?

3) What series is known for the catchphrase "Missed it by that much"?

4) According to a British Film Institute poll of industry professionals in 2000, what is the greatest British television series of all time?

5) What is the name of John Travolta's character on *Welcome Back Kotter*?

6) What is the name of the time traveling scientist on *Quantum Leap*?

7) One of Johnny Depp's early starring roles was on what police show?

8) What is the most widely watched PBS show ever worldwide?

9) In its 2002 list of the 50 greatest television shows of all time, *TV Guide* listed two animated shows, what were they?

10) What show's theme song was the first to hit number one on Billboard's Hot 100?

Quiz 12 Answers

1) George R.R. Martin

2) Dunder Mifflin Paper Company

3) *Get Smart*

4) *Fawlty Towers* – aired 12 episodes in the 1970s

5) Vinnie Barbarino

6) Samuel Beckett

7) *21 Jump Street*

8) *Cosmos* – with Carl Sagan

9) *The Simpsons* and *Rocky and Bullwinkle*

10) *S.W.A.T.* – 1976

Quiz 13

1) In children's television, who is Lumpy Brannum better known as?

2) What is the number of the mobile hospital unit on *M*A*S*H*?

3) What 1960s sitcom was based on the novel *The Fifteenth Pelican*?

4) Who was the only main cast member to be in both the move and television versions of *M*A*S*H*?

5) What was advertised in the first U.S. television commercial?

6) What is the name of Fred Flintstone's paper boy?

7) Who is Underdog in love with?

8) On *Rocky and Bullwinkle*, what is Boris and Natasha's homeland?

9) Who is Dudley Do-Right's nemesis?

10) What is the name of Mr. Peabody's time machine?

Quiz 13 Answers

1) Mr. Green Jeans on *Captain Kangaroo*

2) 4077

3) *The Flying Nun*

4) Gary Burghoff – Radar O'Reilly

5) Bulova watches

6) Arnold

7) Sweet Polly Purebred

8) Pottsylvania

9) Snidely Whiplash

10) Wayback (or WABAC) machine

Quiz 14

1) Charles Addams' *New Yorker* cartoons of a spooky husband and wife were the inspiration for *The Addams Family* and what famous cartoon villain duo?

2) In the original pilot for *Gilligan's Island*, who composed the theme song?

3) In the opening credits for the first season of *Gilligan's Island*, the U.S. flag is at half-mast as the *Minnow* pulls out of harbor; why is the flag at half-mast?

4) What is the name of the Jetson's dog?

5) To capitalize on the popularity of creepy comedies like *The Addams Family* and *The Munsters*, what show introduced Weirdly and Creepella Gruesome as their new neighbors?

6) Fred Flintstone's "Yabba-dabba-doo" was inspired by what well known advertising slogan?

7) The Aunt Harriet character on *Batman* didn't exist in the comics; why was she added to the television show?

8) What is the name of the character played by Angela Lansbury in *Murder, She Wrote*?

9) The character Roger "Race" Bannon appeared as a boy's bodyguard in what cartoon series?

10) On *The Munsters*, what is Lily's maiden name?

Quiz 14 Answers

1) Boris Badenov and Natasha Fatale – *Rocky and Bullwinkle*

2) John Williams – The original song was replaced.

3) John F. Kennedy's assassination – The scene was filmed in

November 1963 in Hawaii; the cast and crew learned of Kennedy's assassination on the last day of filming.

4) Astro

5) *The Flintstones*

6) Brylcreem's "A little dab'll do you" – The mother of the actor who voiced Fred liked to say the Brylcreem slogan, so he suggested it to the creators.

7) To counter rumors that Bruce Wayne and Dick Grayson were gay – They thought adding a female character would round out the household.

8) Jessica Fletcher

9) *Jonny Quest*

10) Dracula

Quiz 15

1) What is Rob and Laura's last name on *The Dick Van Dyke Show*?

2) What is the last name of the family on *Good Times*?

3) On *The Jeffersons*, what is George's business?

4) On *The Wonder Years*, what is Fred Savage's character name?

5) Who played Captain Frank Furillo on *Hill Street Blues*?

6) What is the character name of the Spanish waiter on *Fawlty Towers*?

7) What is the name of the piano playing dog on *The Muppet Show*?

8) What is Bob and Emily's last name on *The Bob Newhart Show*?

9) What is the name of Andy Kaufman's character on *Taxi*?

10) What is the name of the character Betty White played on *The Mary Tyler Moore Show*?

Quiz 15 Answers

1) Petrie

2) Evans

3) Dry cleaning

4) Kevin Arnold

5) Daniel J. Travanti

6) Manuel

7) Rowlf
8) Hartley
9) Latka Gravas
10) Sue Ann Nivens

Quiz 16

1) What is Mary's last name on *The Mary Tyler Moore Show*?
2) What is the name of Tina Fey's character on *30 Rock*?
3) Who was the only American in the group on *Monty Python's Flying Circus*?
4) What recurring character on *The Simpsons* is voiced by Kelsey Grammer?
5) Ted Cassidy, who played Lurch on *The Addams Family*, also played what other role on the show?
6) What cartoon character and gang leader lives in Hoagy's Alley?
7) What is the last name of Woody on *Cheers*?
8) On *Doctor Who*, what planet is the Doctor from?
9) What villain has the real name Oswald Chesterfield Cobblepot?
10) Who played the Lone Ranger in the original series?

Quiz 16 Answers

1) Richards
2) Liz Lemon
3) Terry Gilliam
4) Sideshow Bob
5) Thing – the hand
6) Top Cat
7) Boyd
8) Gallifrey
9) Penguin
10) Clayton Moore

Quiz 17

1) What did the acronym ESPN originally stand for?

2) What is cartoon cat Garfield's favorite food?

3) Poopdeck Pappy is what character's father?

4) What was the first game show broadcast on commercial television?

5) How many points does Bullwinkle have on his antlers?

6) Who is the voice of Marge on *The Simpsons*?

7) What is grandpa Simpson's first name on *The Simpsons*?

8) Who is the first woman to win comedy acting Emmys for three different roles?

9) What was the first streaming series to win the best drama Emmy?

10) What long running children's show had Mr. Do-Bee, a friendly bumblebee who taught children polite behavior, and the Magic Mirror?

Quiz 17 Answers

1) Entertainment and Sports Programming Network

2) Lasagna

3) Popeye

4) *Truth or Consequences* – 1941

5) Six – three on each side

6) Julie Kavner

7) Abraham

8) Julia Louis-Dreyfus – *Seinfeld, The New Adventures of Old Christine, VEEP*

9) *The Handmaid's Tale* – Hulu in 2017

10) *Romper Room* – 1953 to 1994

Quiz 18

1) What 1957-1968 children's show featured a Claymation duo?

2) Who played Maynard G. Krebs on *The Many Loves of Dobie Gillis*?

3) On *The Flying Nun*, what is Sally Field's character's name?

4) On *Bewitched*, what is the name of the character played by Agnes Moorehead?

5) What sitcom features the expression "Well doggies!"?

6) Mr. Peabody was modeled after what actor?

7) What mountain range do the Clampetts of *The Beverly Hillbillies* come from?

8) In what town is *Petticoat Junction* and *Green Acres* set?

9) On *The Munsters*, what is the name of the normal niece?

10) What sportscaster was the host for *ABC's Wide World of Sports*?

Quiz 18 Answers

1) *The Gumby Show* – with his horse Pokey

2) Bob Denver

3) Sister Betrille

4) Endora

5) *The Beverly Hillbillies*

6) Clifton Webb

7) Ozarks

8) Hooterville

9) Marilyn

10) Jim McKay

Quiz 19

1) On *The Munsters*, what is the name of Eddie's pet dragon that lives under the stairs?

2) On *McHale's Navy*, who played the bumbling Ensign Parker?

3) What 1960s show follows the work of Pete Malloy and Jim Reed?

4) Who played the villain Egghead on *Batman*?

5) What 1960s show features Robert Wagner as cat burglar Alexander Mundy?

6) Who was the creator of *The Dick Van Dyke Show* and appeared on the show in a supporting role?

7) On *The Saint*, what is the real name of the character played by Roger Moore?

8) What long running show frequently used the word "wunnerful"?

9) On *F-Troop*, what is the name of the fort?

10) Who created *Jeopardy!* and *Wheel of Fortune*?

Quiz 19 Answers

1) Spot
2) Tim Conway
3) *Adam-12*
4) Vincent Price
5) *It Takes a Thief*
6) Carl Reiner – He appeared as Alan Brady on the show.
7) Simon Templar
8) *The Lawrence Welk Show*
9) Fort Courage
10) Merv Griffin

Quiz 20

1) What are the character first names of the original *My Three Sons*?
2) Who played Herman on *The Munsters*?
3) What is the name of the police detective who chases Dr. Richard Kimble on *The Fugitive*?
4) David Soul and Bobby Sherman played logging brothers on *Here Come the Brides*; where was the show set?
5) What 1969-1972 show was based on a movie of the same name and starred Bill Bixby as a single father raising his son?
6) What 1960s reality show was hosted by Allen Funt and Durward Kirby?
7) What future Oscar winner was a bikini clad go-go dancer on *Rowan & Martin's Laugh-In*?
8) What show features Mike Connors as a Los Angeles private eye?
9) On *Petticoat Junction*, what is the name of the hotel?
10) What future movie star played the role of blacksmith Quint Asper from 1962-1965 on *Gunsmoke*?

Quiz 20 Answers

1) Mike, Robbie, Chip – Ernie joined later after Mike left due to marriage; sister Dodie was added after Steven remarried.
2) Fred Gwynne

3) Lt. Philip Gerard

4) Seattle – based on *Seven Brides for Seven Brothers*

5) *The Courtship of Eddie's Father*

6) *Candid Camera*

7) Goldie Hawn

8) *Mannix*

9) Shady Rest

10) Burt Reynolds

Quiz 21

1) What show opened with "There is nothing wrong with your television set. Do not attempt to adjust the picture"?

2) What 1951–1972 children's show featured science experiments?

3) What is the name of the POW camp on *Hogan Heroes*?

4) What is Wilbur's occupation on *Mr. Ed*?

5) What popular 1957–1963 western was one of the only television shows to spawn a radio show?

6) What is Marlo Thomas' character's name on *That Girl*?

7) Clint Howard appeared with his brother Ron on several episodes of *The Andy Griffith Show* and later starred in what 1960s series?

8) What 1960s show starred Ben Gazzara as a lawyer who is told he only has two years to live?

9) What show featured Clarence, the Cross-Eyed Lion?

10) Who were the actresses who played John Steed's partner on *The Avengers* before and after Diana Rigg?

Quiz 21 Answers

1) *The Outer Limits*

2) *Watch Mr. Wizard*

3) Stalag 13

4) Architect

5) *Have Gun – Will Travel* – The radio show started one year after the television show and reused stories.

6) Ann Marie

7) *Gentle Ben*

8) *Run for Your Life*

9) *Daktari*

10) Honor Blackman (before) and Linda Thorson (after)

Quiz 22

1) In *The Lucy Show*, what is the name of the banker Lucy worked for played by Gale Gordon?

2) What western took place on the Shiloh ranch in Medicine Bow, Wyoming?

3) Who was the director of the St. Louis Zoo and co-host of *Mutual of Omaha's Wild Kingdom*?

4) What western featured the Cannon family in the 1870s Arizona territory?

5) In *The Man from U.N.C.L.E.*, what does U.N.C.L.E. stand for?

6) Who played Kato in *The Green Hornet*?

7) What long running show opened with an animated shoe tapping in time to the theme music?

8) What is Mr. Peabody's first name?

9) What are the names of the twins on *Family Affair*?

10) What 1960s British show had the opening line "I am not a number! I am a free man!"?

Quiz 22 Answers

1) Mr. Mooney

2) *The Virginian*

3) Marlin Perkins

4) *The High Chaparral*

5) United Network Command for Law and Enforcement

6) Bruce Lee

7) *My Three Sons*

8) Hector

9) Buffy and Jody

10) *The Prisoner*

Quiz 23

1) On *Green Acres*, what is Arnold the pig's last name?
2) What show opened with "The story you are about to see is true. The names have been changed to protect the innocent"?
3) On *The Honeymooners*, what is Ed Norton's occupation?
4) What 1952-1966 sitcom featured a real family?
5) What show starts with "A fiery horse with the speed of light, a cloud of dust"?
6) What was the first American series to feature teenagers as the lead characters?
7) What actors play the father and mother in *Father Knows Best*?
8) What character works for Gateman, Goodbury, and Graves Funeral Parlor?
9) What show's main character has business cards showing a chess piece?
10) What early sitcom featured the misadventures of an English teacher at Madison High?

Quiz 23 Answers

1) Ziffel
2) *Dragnet*
3) Sewer worker
4) *The Adventures of Ozzie and Harriet*
5) *The Lone Ranger*
6) *The Many Loves of Dobie Gillis* – 1959
7) Robert Young and Jane Wyatt
8) Herman Munster
9) *Have Gun – Will Travel*
10) *Our Miss Brooks*

Quiz 24

1) On *Bonanza*, Hoss is a nickname; what is the character's real first name?
2) Twenty-two-year-old Warren Beatty got his start playing Milton

Armitage on what sitcom?

3) What is the name of the saloon in *Gunsmoke*?

4) What comedy had a 20-year run with characters like Freddie the Freeloader?

5) What show has the all-time Nielsen season average share rating record?

6) What western features gambling brothers Bret and Bart?

7) Ken Curtis played the deputy on *Gunsmoke* longer than anyone else; what was his full character name?

8) What classic U.S. sitcom was based on the British show *Till Death Us Do Part*?

9) What comedy variety show became a hit with phrases like "The devil made me do it"?

10) What 1970s television family has eight children?

Quiz 24 Answers

1) Eric

2) *The Many Loves of Dobie Gillis*

3) Long Branch

4) *The Red Skelton Show*

5) *I Love Lucy* in 1953 - It had a Nielsen season average share of 67.3 meaning that on average 67.3% of all households viewing television were watching it.

6) *Maverick* – starring James Garner and Jack Kelly

7) Festus Haggen

8) *All in the Family*

9) *The Flip Wilson Show*

10) Bradford – *Eight Is Enough*

Quiz 25

1) What 1970s undercover cop had a cockatoo named Fred?

2) What 1970s show featured Pete, Linc, and Julie solving crimes undercover?

3) Who had the title role in the *All in the Family* spin-off *Maude*?

4) On *Happy Days*, who is the oldest Cunningham child?

5) Before *Three's Company*, John Ritter played a minister on what 1970s drama?

6) What is the name of Ricardo Montalban's character on *Fantasy Island*?

7) What sitcom featured the popular line "Up your nose with a rubber hose"?

8) On *Kojak*, what is Kojak's first name?

9) Where is *The Flying Nun* set?

10) On *The Mary Tyler Moore Show*, what are the call letters of the station where they work?

Quiz 25 Answers

1) *Baretta*

2) *The Mod Squad*

3) Bea Arthur

4) Chuck – He was phased out.

5) *The Waltons*

6) Mr. Roarke

7) *Welcome Back Kotter*

8) Theo

9) Puerto Rico

10) WJM–TV

Quiz 26

1) What 1970s show featured the character Sgt. Pepper Anderson?

2) What is the occupation of Steven Douglas on *My Three Sons*?

3) Who played Tonto in *The Lone Ranger*?

4) Cloris Leachman starred in a spin-off from *The Mary Tyler Moore Show*; what is the name of the character she played?

5) What is John Cleese's full character name in *Fawlty Towers*?

6) In the 1970s show *Chico and the Man*, Freddie Prinze played Chico; who played the man?

7) What sitcom featured a never seen character Carlton the doorman?

8) The actor who voiced the title character on the animated series *Jonny Quest* was 17 at the time and went on to a long acting career;

who is he?

9) What is the name of Dennis the Menace's dog?

10) Who played *The Fugitive*?

Quiz 26 Answers

1) *Police Woman* – starring Angie Dickinson

2) Aeronautical engineer

3) Jay Silverheels

4) Phyllis Lindstrom

5) Basil Fawlty

6) Jack Albertson

7) *Rhoda*

8) Tim Matheson

9) Ruff

10) David Janssen

Quiz 27

1) Ringo Starr narrated what children's show?

2) James Drury had the title role in what western series?

3) Benjamin Kubelsky gained fame as what comedian?

4) What fictional character has been played by the most actors on film and television?

5) On *The Beverly Hillbillies*, who is Mr. Drysdale's secretary?

6) Color television was first successfully transmitted in the U.S. in what year?

7) On *Star Trek*, who played Ensign Chekov?

8) Where do Rocky and Bullwinkle live?

9) On *M*A*S*H*, what is Radar's favorite drink?

10) Wo Fat is the enemy of what detective?

Quiz 27 Answers

1) *Thomas the Tank Engine*

2) *The Virginian*

3) Jack Benny

4) Sherlock Holmes

5) Jane Hathaway

6) 1953

7) Walter Koenig

8) Frostbite Falls, Minnesota

9) Grape Nehi

10) Steve McGarrett - *Hawaii Five-O*

Quiz 28

1) Roy Thinnes played David Vincent in what 1960s science fiction series?

2) How many seconds elapsed before the tape self-destructed on *Mission Impossible*?

3) Who sang the theme song to *Rawhide*?

4) What is Clint Eastwood's character name on *Rawhide*?

5) How long was the original mission of Star Trek's Enterprise supposed to be?

6) Who is the head news writer for WJM-TV?

7) Where does Yogi bear live?

8) What is the name of the Douglas' family dog on *My Three Sons*?

9) **What character did Chuck Connors play on *The Rifleman*?**

10) Who was the first woman to anchor a U.S. network evening newscast?

Quiz 28 Answers

1) *The Invaders*

2) Five seconds

3) Frankie Laine

4) Rowdy Yates

5) Five years

6) Murray Slaughter – *The Mary Tyler Moore Show*

7) Jellystone Park

8) Tramp

9) Lucas McCain

10) Barbara Walters

Quiz 29

1) Who made the Rolling Stones sing "Let's spend the night together" as "Let's spend some time together"?
2) What is Beaver Cleaver's real first name?
3) What character did McLean Stevenson play on *M*A*S*H*?
4) Who took dictation from Perry Mason?
5) Who hosted *Night Gallery*?
6) Who is the Ponderosa's Chinese cook?
7) What is Mickey Mouse's dog's name?
8) **Where is Bullwinkle Moose originally from?**
9) Who used to ask, "Hey, Eddie, kees me goodnight"?
10) Who played Sally Rogers on *The Dick Van Dyke Show*?

Quiz 29 Answers

1) Ed Sullivan
2) Theodore
3) Henry Blake
4) Della Street
5) Rod Serling
6) Hop Sing
7) Pluto
8) **Moosylvania – It is a small island in Lake of the Woods that neither the U.S. nor Canada wants to claim.**
9) Topo Gigio – Italian mouse puppet who appeared on *The Ed Sullivan Show*
10) Rose Marie

Quiz 30

1) What character was a knight without armor in a savage land?
2) Who played Captain Kangaroo?
3) What long time *60 Minutes* correspondent hosted seven game shows early in his career?

4) Who was the first woman to host *Saturday Night Live?*

5) Who played Doc Adams on *Gunsmoke?*

6) What sitcom ran the most first run episodes in the 1990s?

7) What major cable network put on a polka festival as its first attempt at original programming?

8) When danger appeared, Quick Draw McGraw became what super hero?

9) What 1980s series starred Bruce Willis in a detective agency?

10) *Happy Days* was a spin-off from what show?

Quiz 30 Answers

1) Paladin – from *Have Gun - Will Travel*

2) Bob Keeshan

3) Mike Wallace

4) Candace Bergen – 1975

5) Milburn Stone

6) *The Simpsons*

7) HBO

8) El Kabong

9) *Moonlighting*

10) *Love American Style*

U.S. Geography

Quiz 1

1) What is the largest city on the Mississippi River?
2) What is the oldest city in the U.S.?
3) What is the name of the island between the two waterfalls at Niagara Falls?
4) What is the highest waterfall in the U.S.?
5) What is the least populous state capital?
6) What major city is named after a U.S. vice president of the 1840s?
7) What state has the largest area of inland water?
8) Which of the 48 contiguous states extends farthest north?
9) What state's three most populous cities all have names beginning with the letter C?
10) What is the least accessible state capital?

Quiz 1 Answers

1) Memphis, Tennessee
2) St. Augustine, Florida – 1565
3) Goat Island
4) Yosemite Falls – 2,425 feet
5) Montpelier, Vermont
6) Dallas – George Mifflin Dallas was vice president for James K. Polk.
7) Alaska
8) Minnesota
9) Ohio – Columbus, Cleveland, Cincinnati
10) Juneau Alaska – fly or take a boat

Quiz 2

1) The Statue of Liberty stands on what island?
2) What is the largest island in the contiguous 48 states?
3) How many miles separate the U.S. and Cuba?

4) What state has a Union Jack on its flag?

5) What is the only borough of New York City that is not mainly on an island?

6) What state capital is named after a famous German statesman?

7) What state is the geographic center of North America?

8) What state is closest to Bermuda?

9) In the 48 contiguous states, what is the largest city based on land area?

10) What is the second largest wine producing state?

Quiz 2 Answers

1) Liberty Island

2) Long Island

3) 90

4) Hawaii

5) Bronx

6) Bismarck, North Dakota – after Otto von Bismarck

7) North Dakota

8) North Carolina

9) Jacksonville, Florida – 758 square miles

10) Washington

Quiz 3

1) What national park has the nickname "Crown of the Continent"?

2) What is the only state with a one syllable name?

3) By area, what is the third largest state?

4) What is the only state with the same name as a country?

5) How many state capitals are named after presidents?

6) What state capital has the largest population?

7) What is the highest peak east of the Mississippi River?

8) What two state capitals include the name of the state?

9) What is the only state flag that has an image of a president?

10) What is the most densely populated state?

Quiz 3 Answers

1) Glacier National Park
2) Maine
3) California
4) Georgia
5) Four – Lincoln, Jefferson City, Jackson, Madison
6) Phoenix, Arizona
7) Mount Mitchell – 6,684 feet in North Carolina
8) Oklahoma City and Indianapolis
9) Washington
10) New Jersey

Quiz 4

1) In the 48 contiguous states, what is the most northern state capital?
2) What is the deepest gorge in the U.S.?
3) How many states border the Gulf of Mexico?
4) What are the five boroughs of New York City?
5) What state has the most counties?
6) What is the tallest volcano in the contiguous 48 states?
7) What is the only non-rectangular state flag?
8) How many states border the Atlantic Ocean (excluding the Gulf of Mexico)?
9) What is the oldest city west of the Rocky Mountains?
10) What state has the fewest counties?

Quiz 4 Answers

1) Olympia, Washington
2) Hells Canyon – 7,993 feet deep on the Snake River on the Oregon and Idaho border
3) Five – Florida, Alabama, Mississippi, Louisiana, Texas
4) Bronx, Queens, Staten Island, Manhattan, Brooklyn
5) Texas – 254

6) Mount Rainier – 14,411 feet in Washington

7) Ohio – swallowtail design

8) 14 – Maine, New Hampshire, Massachusetts, Rhode Island, Connecticut, New York, New Jersey, Delaware, Maryland, Virginia, North Carolina, South Carolina, Georgia, Florida

9) Astoria, Oregon - 1811

10) Delaware – three

Quiz 5

1) What is the most visited U.S. national park?

2) What state is the geographic center of the 48 contiguous states?

3) What is the only state that ends with a "K"?

4) By area, what is the largest U.S. city?

5) What is the highest elevation state capital?

6) Fort Knox is in what state?

7) What is the only state that borders just one other state?

8) What two state capitals are named for royalty?

9) What is the only two-sided state flag (different designs on each side)?

10) How many states share a land or water border with Canada?

Quiz 5 Answers

1) Great Smoky Mountains

2) Kansas

3) New York

4) Yakutat, Alaska – 9,459 square miles

5) Santa Fe, New Mexico – 7,000 feet

6) Kentucky

7) Maine

8) Annapolis, Maryland and Albany, New York – They were named for Princess Anne of Denmark and Norway who became Queen of England and for the Duke of York and Albany who became King James II of England.

9) Oregon

10) 13 - Alaska, Washington, Idaho, Montana, North Dakota, Minnesota, Michigan, Ohio, Pennsylvania, New York, Vermont, New Hampshire, Maine

Quiz 6

1) How many states don't border either the ocean or one of the Great Lakes?
2) What three rivers meet in Pittsburgh?
3) What is the flattest state?
4) What is the only two-word state capital in a two-word state?
5) The Mississippi river runs through or along how many states?
6) What two state capitals sit on the borders of other states?
7) What is the only state name that doesn't share any letters with its capital city?
8) What is the only state capital without a McDonald's?
9) What two state capitals are located on the Mississippi River?
10) In the 48 contiguous states, what is the most southern state capital?

Quiz 6 Answers

1) 20 - Arizona, Arkansas, Colorado, Idaho, Iowa, Kansas, Kentucky, Missouri, Montana, Nebraska, Nevada, New Mexico, North Dakota, Oklahoma, South Dakota, Tennessee, Utah, Vermont, West Virginia, Wyoming
2) Allegheny, Monongahela, Ohio
3) Florida – 345 feet between its highest and lowest points
4) Santa Fe, New Mexico
5) 10 – Arkansas, Illinois, Iowa, Kentucky, Louisiana, Minnesota, Mississippi, Missouri, Tennessee, Wisconsin
6) Carson City, Nevada (California border) and Trenton, New Jersey (Pennsylvania border)
7) South Dakota – Pierre
8) Montpelier, Vermont
9) St. Paul and Baton Rouge
10) Austin, Texas

Quiz 7

1) What is the only state name that can be typed on one row of a standard keyboard?
2) What is the largest island in the U.S.?
3) What is the most visited U.S. city?
4) What is the only state on the east coast to fall partly in the central time zone?
5) What state has the highest per capita income?
6) What state has the highest percentage foreign born population?
7) What state has the lowest median age?
8) What state has the highest median age?
9) What state has the largest number of active volcanoes?
10) What is the westernmost state?

Quiz 7 Answers

1) Alaska
2) Hawaii
3) Orlando, Florida - New York City is second.
4) Florida
5) Connecticut
6) California
7) Utah
8) Maine
9) Alaska – 130 out of the 169 active volcanoes in the U.S.
10) Alaska

Quiz 8

1) What state has the most miles of rivers?
2) What state has the most national parks?
3) What state has the highest percentage of federal land?
4) What two states share the longest border?
5) How many states refer to themselves as commonwealths in their names?

6) What state capital was once the national capital?

7) What U.S. state is closest to Africa?

8) What is the only letter that doesn't appear in any state name?

9) What is the longest state from north to south?

10) At its closest point, what is the distance between the U.S. and Russia?

Quiz 8 Answers

1) Nebraska – major rivers include Platte, Niobrara, Missouri, Republican

2) California – nine

3) Nevada – 81%

4) Texas and Oklahoma – 700 miles

5) Four – Kentucky, Massachusetts, Pennsylvania, Virginia - There is no legal distinction just a naming difference from earlier times.

6) Annapolis, Maryland

7) Maine – Quoddy Head peninsula is 3,154 miles from Morocco.

8) Q

9) Alaska – 1,479 miles

10) 2.4 miles

Quiz 9

1) How many U.S. states are larger than the United Kingdom?

2) How many states have land farther south than the most northern point of Mexico?

3) At one point in the year, it is the same local time for parts of Oregon and Florida; how is this possible?

4) What is the official language of the U.S.?

5) What was the original name for the island where the Statue of Liberty stands?

6) New York City has a larger population than how many states?

7) What is the only major U.S. city founded by a woman?

8) How many states are at least partly north of the southernmost point of Canada?

9) What is the second largest island in the U.S.?

10) What Canadian province borders the most states?

Quiz 9 Answers

1) 11 – Alaska, Texas, California, Montana, New Mexico, Arizona, Nevada, Colorado, Oregon, Wyoming, Michigan

2) 11 – Alabama, Arizona, California, Florida, Georgia, Hawaii, Louisiana, Mississippi, New Mexico, South Carolina, Texas

3) A small part of eastern Oregon is in the mountain time zone, and a small part of western Florida is in the central time zone. When the change from daylight saving time to standard time is made, these two areas share the same time for one hour after the central time zone has fallen back to standard time and before the mountain time zone has.

4) There isn't one.

5) Bedloe's Island

6) 39

7) Miami – Julia Tuttle

8) 27 – Alaska, California, Connecticut, Idaho, Illinois, Indiana, Iowa, Maine, Massachusetts, Michigan, Minnesota, Montana, Nebraska, Nevada, New Hampshire, New York, North Dakota, Ohio, Oregon, Pennsylvania, Rhode Island, South Dakota, Utah, Vermont, Washington, Wisconsin, Wyoming

9) Kodiak Island, Alaska – 3,672 square miles

10) Ontario – borders Minnesota, Michigan, Ohio, Pennsylvania, New York

Quiz 10

1) In the 48 contiguous states, what is the most western state capital?

2) How many states does the Canadian province of Alberta border?

3) What state has the highest lowest elevation point?

4) By area, what is the largest lake entirely within the U.S.?

5) By area, what is the largest lake entirely within one state?

6) What state has the lowest highest elevation point?

7) What two states have a lowest elevation point below sea level?

8) By area, what is the fourth largest state?

9) Which of the contiguous 48 states has the longest border with

Canada?

10) What were the last four states to join the U.S.?

Quiz 10 Answers

1) Olympia, Washington
2) One – Montana
3) Colorado – 3,315 feet
4) Lake Michigan
5) Great Salt Lake
6) Florida – 345 feet
7) California and Louisiana
8) Montana
9) Michigan
10) New Mexico, Arizona, Alaska, Hawaii

Quiz 11

1) What is the most commonly occurring place name in the U.S.?
2) By area, what is the largest state east of the Mississippi River?
3) What is the source of the Mississippi River?
4) What New Mexico resort town was named after a radio game show?
5) By area, what is the smallest state?
6) How many states border the Great Lakes?
7) What is the highest mountain in the U.S.?
8) What is the highest mountain in the contiguous 48 states?
9) What state capital is 10 miles from Princeton University?
10) What is the only state name that ends in three vowels?

Quiz 11 Answers

1) Washington
2) Georgia
3) Lake Itasca, Minnesota
4) Truth or Consequences
5) Rhode Island

6) Eight - Illinois, Indiana, Michigan, Minnesota, New York, Ohio, Pennsylvania, Wisconsin

7) Denali or Mount McKinley, Alaska – 20,310 feet

8) Mount Whitney, California – 14,505 feet

9) Trenton, New Jersey

10) Hawaii

Quiz 12

1) What state receives the least sunshine?

2) What is the southernmost state?

3) After Canada and Mexico, what country is closest to the U.S.?

4) How many states border California?

5) What two states share the most borders with other states?

6) What state has the lowest average elevation?

7) How many states are at least partially north of the southernmost part of Canada and at least partially south of the northernmost point of Mexico?

8) What state has the longest border with Canada?

9) How many states border the Pacific Ocean?

10) What was the first state with a woman governor?

Quiz 12 Answers

1) Alaska

2) Hawaii

3) Russia – 2.4 miles

4) Three – Oregon, Nevada, Arizona

5) Missouri and Tennessee – eight states border each

6) Delaware – 60 feet average elevation

7) One – California

8) Alaska

9) Five – Washington, Oregon, California, Alaska, Hawaii

10) Wyoming – 1925

Quiz 13

1) What state has the least rainfall?
2) What landmark became 1,313 feet shorter in 1980?
3) What is the only state that borders a Canadian territory?
4) How many states border Mexico?
5) What state has the second longest coastline?
6) What four states have active volcanoes?
7) What city has the only royal palace in the U.S.?
8) What state has the most rainfall?
9) What is the easternmost state capital?
10) What is the easternmost state?

Quiz 13 Answers

1) Nevada – 9.5 inches mean annual precipitation
2) Mount St. Helens
3) Alaska
4) Four – California, Arizona, New Mexico, and Texas
5) Florida
6) Alaska, California, Hawaii, Washington
7) Honolulu, Hawaii
8) Hawaii – 63.7 inches mean annual precipitation
9) Augusta, Maine
10) Alaska – stretches into the Eastern Hemisphere

Quiz 14

1) What state capital has the largest land area?
2) What state capital has more than 30 Buddhist temples?
3) What state has the highest average elevation?
4) What state has the smallest population?
5) What is the largest U.S. city on the Great Lakes?
6) What is the only state that ends with three consonants?
7) What state has the most tornadoes on average?

8) Where is the lowest elevation land point in the U.S.?

9) What is the deepest lake in the U.S.?

10) By area, what is the smallest state west of the Mississippi River?

Quiz 14 Answers

1) Juneau, Alaska – 3,255 square miles

2) Honolulu, Hawaii

3) Colorado – 6,800 feet average

4) Wyoming

5) Chicago

6) Massachusetts

7) Texas

8) Death Valley, California – 279 feet below sea level

9) Crater Lake – 1,949 feet

10) Hawaii

Quiz 15

1) What Is the most popular street name in the U.S.?

2) By volume, what is the largest lake entirely within the U.S.?

3) Of the 10 tallest mountains in the U.S., how many are in Alaska?

4) By volume, what is the largest lake entirely within one state?

5) What state has the highest percent of its area that is water?

6) What state has the lowest percent of its area that is water?

7) How many states are entirely north of the southernmost point of Canada?

8) By area, what state has the largest county?

9) By population, what state has the largest county?

10) What state had the first commercial oil well in the U.S.?

Quiz 15 Answers

1) Park

2) Lake Michigan

3) 10 – Mt. Whitney, the highest peak in the contiguous 48 states, is the 11th highest in the U.S.

4) Lake Iliamna, Alaska

5) Michigan – followed by Hawaii and Rhode Island

6) New Mexico – followed by Arizona and Colorado

7) 13 - Alaska, Washington, Oregon, Idaho, Montana, North Dakota, South Dakota, Minnesota, Wisconsin, Michigan, Vermont, New Hampshire, Maine

8) California – San Bernardino county is 20,105 square miles.

9) California – Los Angeles county

10) Pennsylvania

Quiz 16

1) At the start of the 20th century, how many U.S. states were there?

2) What was the first U.S. state?

3) What was the first U.S. national monument?

4) What is the oldest U.S. state capital?

5) What two states donated land to create Washington, D.C.?

6) What is the highest peak between the Rocky Mountains and the Appalachian Mountains?

7) The border between what two states is partially formed by the Continental Divide?

8) What state's southern border is formed by a river of the same name?

9) What two Canadian provinces only border one state?

10) What is the longest interstate highway?

Quiz 16 Answers

1) 45 – Oklahoma, New Mexico, Arizona, Alaska, and Hawaii weren't states yet.

2) Delaware – December 7, 1787

3) Devils Tower, Wyoming – 1906

4) Santa Fe, New Mexico – 1609

5) Maryland and Virginia

6) Mount Magazine – 2,753 feet in the Ouachita Mountains in Arkansas

7) Idaho and Montana

8) Ohio

9) Alberta and New Brunswick

10) I-90 from Boston to Seattle – 3,111 miles

Quiz 17

1) How many national capital cities were there before Washington, D.C.?

2) What state has the only active diamond mine?

3) By area, what is the second largest lake entirely within the U.S.?

4) What state has the longest coastline?

5) What three states have their eastern and western borders entirely defined by water?

6) What is the widest state from east to west?

7) What four states meet at Four Corners?

8) How many states have never elected a female governor, U.S. senator, or U.S. representative?

9) How many different capital cities has Texas had as a republic and state?

10) What year did New Mexico and Arizona become the 47th and 48th states?

Quiz 17 Answers

1) Eight – Philadelphia, Baltimore, Lancaster, York, Princeton, Annapolis, Trenton, New York City

2) Arkansas

3) Great Salt Lake

4) Alaska

5) Hawaii, Florida, Iowa

6) Alaska – 2,400 miles

7) New Mexico, Arizona, Colorado, Utah

8) Zero – Mississippi was the last remaining state until they elected a female U.S. representative in 2018.

9) 12 – including Galveston, Houston, Austin

10) 1912

U.S. Presidents

Quiz 1

1) Who is the only president to serve two nonconsecutive terms?
2) Who was the first president to attend Monday night football?
3) Who was the last president with facial hair?
4) Who was the first president born in a hospital?
5) What president twice served as an executioner?
6) Who are the only two first ladies born outside the U.S.?
7) Who was the first president to live in the White House?
8) Who is the only president born on the Fourth of July?
9) What first lady refused secret service coverage and was given her own gun?
10) Who was the first president to have been divorced?

Quiz 1 Answers

1) Grover Cleveland - 22nd and 24th president
2) Jimmy Carter
3) William Howard Taft
4) Jimmy Carter
5) Grover Cleveland – in his duty as sheriff
6) Louisa Adams and Melania Trump
7) John Adams
8) Calvin Coolidge
9) Eleanor Roosevelt
10) Ronald Reagan

Quiz 2

1) Who is the youngest ever president?
2) Who was the first president depicted on a circulating U.S. monetary coin?
3) What president's mother had the first name Stanley?

4) What didn't president James Buchanan have that every other president has had?

5) What president's wife saw him elected but died before his inauguration?

6) What two first lady's husbands and sons both served as U.S. president?

7) Who gave Caroline Kennedy her dog Pushinska while her dad was president?

8) What president had the most children?

9) What president had the shortest term?

10) What president was shot at twice at point-blank range but survived because both guns misfired?

Quiz 2 Answers

1) Theodore Roosevelt – 42

2) Abraham Lincoln

3) Barack Obama

4) A wife – He never married, and many historians speculate that he may have been the first gay president.

5) Andrew Jackson

6) Barbara Bush and Abigail Adams

7) Nikita Khrushchev

8) John Tyler – 15 by two wives

9) William Henry Harrison – 31 days - He caught a cold on inauguration day that turned into a fatal case of pneumonia. His grandson Benjamin would later also be president.

10) Andrew Jackson – first presidential assassination attempt

Quiz 3

1) What does the S stand for in Harry S. Truman?

2) Who was the only president to get married at the White House?

3) Who was the heaviest president?

4) What president remarried his wife three years after their wedding because her first divorce wasn't finalized?

5) What is the most common first name of presidents?

6) Who was the tallest president?

7) Who was the shortest president?

8) Who is the only man to have been both Chief Justice of the U.S. Supreme Court and president?

9) What president is commonly credited with inventing the swivel chair?

10) Who was the first president born outside the original 13 states?

Quiz 3 Answers

1) Nothing – The S was in honor of both of his grandfathers but didn't stand for a middle name.

2) Grover Cleveland

3) William Howard Taft – about 340 pounds when he left office

4) Andrew Jackson

5) James – six presidents

6) Abraham Lincoln – 6 feet 4 inches

7) James Madison – 5 feet 4 inches

8) William Howard Taft

9) Thomas Jefferson

10) Abraham Lincoln

Quiz 4

1) At president Andrew Jackson's funeral in 1845, who was removed for swearing?

2) Who was the first president to ride in an automobile while in office?

3) Who was the only president to be held as a prisoner of war?

4) What president was the first to use the Oval Office?

5) Who was the first president to fly on official business?

6) What president enacted the law requiring cigarette manufacturers to put health warnings on their packages?

7) Who are the only two men who have run effectively unopposed for president?

8) What president tried to create the "Great Society"?

9) What president said, "Forgive your enemies, but never forget their

names"?

10) What president wrote 37 books?

Quiz 4 Answers

1) His pet parrot

2) Theodore Roosevelt

3) Andrew Jackson – He joined the Revolutionary War at age 13 and was captured by the British.

4) William Howard Taft – He made the West Wing a permanent building and had the Oval Office built.

5) Franklin D. Roosevelt - 1943 secret trip to Casablanca

6) Lyndon B. Johnson

7) George Washington and James Monroe

8) Lyndon B. Johnson – set of domestic programs to eliminate poverty and racial injustice

9) John F. Kennedy

10) Theodore Roosevelt

Quiz 5

1) Who is the only president ever granted a patent?

2) Who was the editor of the magazine *Babies Just Babies* when her husband was elected president?

3) Who was the first president to be photographed at his inauguration?

4) Who was the first vice president to become president upon the death of a president?

5) Three first ladies are tied as the tallest at 5 feet 11 inches; who are they?

6) What two presidents died on July 4, 1826?

7) What president had a raccoon for a pet while in the White House?

8) Who is the oldest person to win a presidential election?

9) Who was the first Roman Catholic vice president?

10) Who is the youngest ever elected president?

Quiz 5 Answers

1) Abraham Lincoln - a device that helped buoy vessels over shoals
2) Eleanor Roosevelt
3) James Buchanan
4) John Tyler – He succeeded William Henry Harrison who died of pneumonia 31 days after inauguration.
5) Melania Trump, Michelle Obama, Eleanor Roosevelt
6) Thomas Jefferson and John Adams
7) Calvin Coolidge – The raccoon was a gift and was supposed to be served for Thanksgiving dinner; Coolidge made it a pet and even walked it on a leash on the White House grounds.
8) Ronald Reagan – 73 at time of his re-election
9) Joseph Biden
10) John F. Kennedy - 43

Quiz 6

1) Who was the first president to win a Nobel Prize?
2) Which president was a Rhodes Scholar?
3) Which first lady was later elected to public office?
4) Who was the only president not elected president or vice president?
5) What is the most common birth state for presidents?
6) What president signed Father's Day into law?
7) Who was the only Eagle Scout president?
8) Who was the first vice president who didn't go on to become president?
9) What president was born as Leslie Lynch King Jr.?
10) Who was the first president to govern over all 50 states?

Quiz 6 Answers

1) Theodore Roosevelt
2) Bill Clinton
3) Hilary Clinton
4) Gerald Ford

5) Virginia – eight
6) Lyndon B. Johnson
7) Gerald Ford
8) Aaron Burr – third vice president
9) Gerald Ford
10) Dwight D. Eisenhower

Quiz 7

1) What president was a head cheerleader in high school?
2) Who was the first president to declare war?
3) Who was the first president to be impeached?
4) Who was vice president when Abraham Lincoln was assassinated?
5) Who was the youngest first lady ever?
6) Who was the first president to leave the U.S. while in office?
7) How many presidents were only children?
8) Who was the only president to win a Pulitzer Prize?
9) How many presidents have won the Nobel Peace Prize?
10) What president imposed the first federal income tax?

Quiz 7 Answers

1) George W. Bush
2) James Madison – War of 1812
3) Andrew Johnson – 1868
4) Andrew Johnson
5) Frances Folsom Cleveland – She was 21 when she married Grover Cleveland in the White House; he was 49.
6) Theodore Roosevelt – He went to Panama to inspect canal construction.
7) Zero
8) John F. Kennedy – for *Profiles in Courage*
9) Four – Theodore Roosevelt, Woodrow Wilson, Jimmy Carter, Barack Obama
10) Abraham Lincoln

Quiz 8

1) Who was the only president with a PhD?
2) Who was the only president to never sign a bill into law?
3) Who was the first republican president?
4) Who was the first president to appear on television?
5) What two presidents were Quakers?
6) Who was the first president paid a salary of $100,000 or more?
7) Who was president when electricity was installed in the White House?
8) Who was president when running water was installed in the White House?
9) What president had a special bathtub big enough to hold four men installed in the White House?
10) How many presidents never attended college?

Quiz 8 Answers

1) Woodrow Wilson – history and political science
2) William Henry Harrison – 31 days as president
3) Abraham Lincoln
4) Franklin D. Roosevelt
5) Herbert Hoover and Richard Nixon
6) Harry S. Truman
7) Benjamin Harrison – 1889
8) Andrew Jackson - 1833
9) William Howard Taft
10) Nine – Washington, Jackson, Van Buren, Taylor, Fillmore, Lincoln, Andrew Johnson, Cleveland, Truman

Quiz 9

1) Who was the first president born outside the contiguous 48 states?
2) How many presidents were born as British subjects?
3) What is the most common religious affiliation for presidents?
4) How many presidents have been left handed?

5) How many presidents served as vice presidents?

6) What president was in office when the term "first lady" was first used?

7) How many presidents were assassinated in office?

8) How many presidents died in office?

9) How many presidential candidates have won the popular vote but lost the election?

10) What president lived the longest?

Quiz 9 Answers

1) Barack Obama

2) Eight – Washington, John Adams, Jefferson, Madison, Monroe, John Quincy Adams, Jackson, William Henry Harrison

3) Episcopalian

4) Eight – Garfield, Hoover, Truman, Ford, Reagan, G.W. Bush, Clinton, Obama

5) 14

6) Rutherford B. Hayes – 1877

7) Four – Lincoln, Garfield, McKinley, Kennedy

8) Eight – Harrison, Taylor, Lincoln, Garfield, McKinley, Harding, Franklin D. Roosevelt, Kennedy

9) Four – Andrew Jackson against John Quincy Adams, Samuel Tilden against Rutherford B. Hayes, Al Gore against George W. Bush, and Hilary Clinton against Donald Trump

10) Gerald Ford – 93; Reagan was also 93 but was 45 days younger.

Quiz 10

1) What president died at the youngest age?

2) What first lady lived the longest?

3) Who was the oldest first lady at time of inauguration?

4) How many first ladies have died while their husband was in office?

5) Who was the only president who had been a union leader?

6) What three presidents have won Grammys for best spoken word album?

7) How many elected vice presidents became president for the first

time through election?

8) How many presidents didn't have a wife when they took office?

9) What president worked as a lifeguard?

10) What president sent Lewis and Clark on their expedition?

Quiz 10 Answers

1) John F. Kennedy – 46

2) Bess Truman – 97

3) Barbara Bush – 63

4) Three – Tyler, Harrison, Wilson

5) Ronald Reagan – president of the Screen Actors Guild

6) Clinton, Carter, Obama

7) Two – Martin Van Buren and George H.W. Bush - Originally, the vice president wasn't elected separately.

8) Six – Jefferson, Jackson, Van Buren, and Arthur were all widowers; Cleveland married while in office; Buchanan never married.

9) Ronald Reagan

10) Thomas Jefferson

Quiz 11

1) Who was the first president to visit Alaska?

2) What was George Washington's first occupation?

3) Who was the first U.S. senator to serve as president?

4) Who was the first governor to serve as president?

5) Who won the first presidential election after the 26th amendment gave 18-year-olds the right to vote?

6) What president was known as "The Great Engineer"?

7) What president created the Drug Enforcement Agency?

8) What president was known as "The Trust Buster"?

9) Who was the first sitting president to visit Hiroshima?

10) James Buchanan was morally opposed to slavery but believed it was protected by the constitution, so what did he do?

Quiz 11 Answers

1) Warren Harding – 1923
2) Surveyor
3) James Madison
4) Jimmy Carter
5) Richard Nixon
6) Herbert Hoover – He was a mining engineer who worked around the world and had a large engineering consulting company.
7) Richard Nixon
8) Theodore Roosevelt
9) Barack Obama
10) He bought slaves with his own money and freed them.

Quiz 12

1) When accused of being two-faced, what president said, "If I had two faces, would I be wearing this one?"
2) Franklin D. Roosevelt was the first president to use an armored car; who did the car previously belong to?
3) What religious holiday was Abraham Lincoln assassinated on?
4) Who was the first president born in the U.S.?
5) What was Ronald Reagan's pet name for Nancy?
6) Under the original terms of the U.S. Constitution, the president didn't choose his own vice president; how was it decided?
7) When president Truman visited Disneyland in 1957, why did he refuse to go on the Dumbo ride?
8) What physical trait did George Washington, Thomas Jefferson, Andrew Jackson, Martin Van Buren, and Dwight Eisenhower have in common?
9) Who was the first president born in the 20th century?
10) What president signed the treaty to purchase Alaska from Russia?

Quiz 12 Answers

1) Abraham Lincoln
2) Al Capone

3) Good Friday

4) Martin Van Buren – eighth president

5) Mommy poo pants

6) The candidate with the second most electoral votes was vice president.

7) As a Democrat, he didn't want to be seen riding in the symbol of the Republican party.

8) Redheads

9) John F. Kennedy

10) Andrew Johnson

Quiz 13

1) Walt Whitman's poem "O Captain! My Captain!" was written about what president?

2) How many future presidents signed the Declaration of Independence?

3) Who was the only president who earned an MBA degree?

4) In what city was president McKinley assassinated?

5) What disease did John F. Kennedy contract as a young child?

6) Who was the first president to campaign by telephone?

7) Who was the first president to call the presidential residence the White House?

8) What U.S. president weighed the least?

9) Who was the first president to ride a railroad while in office?

10) What constitutional amendment limits the president to two terms?

Quiz 13 Answers

1) Abraham Lincoln – It was written after Lincoln's assassination.

2) Two – John Adams and Thomas Jefferson

3) George W. Bush

4) Buffalo, New York

5) Scarlet fever

6) William McKinley

7) Theodore Roosevelt

8) James Madison – 100 pounds

9) Andrew Jackson

10) 22nd

Quiz 14

1) Who was the last president who wasn't either a Democrat or Republican?

2) According to his wife, what was Abraham Lincoln's hobby?

3) Who was the first president to run against a woman candidate?

4) Originally, people bowed to the U.S. president; who was the first president to shake hands rather than bowing?

5) Who was the first president to attend a baseball game?

6) George Washington, John Adams, and Thomas Jefferson were all avid collectors and players of what game?

7) Who was the first president to visit all 50 states?

8) Who was the first president to have a beard?

9) What president was once a fashion model?

10) What president collected *Spiderman* and *Conan the Barbarian* comic books?

Quiz 14 Answers

1) Millard Fillmore – 1850

2) Cats – He loved them and could play with them for hours; he once allowed a cat to eat from the table at a formal White House dinner.

3) Ulysses S. Grant – Virginia Woodhull was a nominee of the Equal Rights Party in 1872.

4) Thomas Jefferson

5) Benjamin Harrison – 1892

6) Marbles

7) Richard Nixon

8) Abraham Lincoln

9) Gerald Ford – *Cosmopolitan* and *Look* magazines in the 1940s

10) Barack Obama

Quiz 15

1) Who was the first president who was a Boy Scout?
2) What president served in the U.S. House of Representatives after he served as president?
3) How many presidents regularly wore beards while in office?
4) What president was the first to have a child born in the White House?
5) Who was the first president born west of the Mississippi River?
6) Who was the only president who made his own clothes?
7) Who was the only president to serve in both the Revolutionary War and the War of 1812?
8) What president had the largest feet?
9) What Christmas item did Theodore Roosevelt ban from the White House?
10) Who was the first Navy veteran to become president?

Quiz 15 Answers

1) John F. Kennedy
2) John Quincy Adams
3) Five – Lincoln, Grant, Hayes, Garfield, Benjamin Harrison
4) Grover Cleveland – 1893
5) Herbert Hoover – Iowa
6) Andrew Johnson – He had been a tailor's apprentice and opened his own tailor shop; he made his own clothes most of his life.
7) Andrew Jackson
8) Warren G. Harding – size 14
9) Christmas trees – He had environmental concerns.
10) John F. Kennedy

Quiz 16

1) What five surnames have been shared by more than one president?
2) Who was the only president that never lived in Washington, D.C.?
3) What president was the target of two assassination attempts in 17 days?

4) What president had the largest personal book collection in the U.S. and sold it to become part of the Library of Congress?

5) What play was Abraham Lincoln watching when he was assassinated?

6) Who was the first president inaugurated in Washington, D.C.?

7) Who was the first president with no prior elected political experience?

8) Who was the first president to travel in a car, plane, and submarine?

9) Who was president when the first U.S. national park was created?

10) Who was the first president to hold a televised news conference?

Quiz 16 Answers

1) Adams, Harrison, Johnson, Roosevelt, Bush

2) George Washington

3) Gerald Ford

4) Thomas Jefferson

5) *Our American Cousin*

6) Thomas Jefferson

7) Zachary Taylor – 12th president and Mexican-American War general

8) Theodore Roosevelt

9) Ulysses S. Grant – Yellowstone was the first national park in the world.

10) Dwight D. Eisenhower

World Geography

Quiz 1

1) What country are the Galapagos Islands part of?
2) What is the highest mountain in the Western Hemisphere?
3) What kind of animal are the Canary Islands named after?
4) What country has the longest land border?
5) What is the world's third most populous country?
6) Easter Island is a territory of what country?
7) By area, what is the second largest lake in North America?
8) What is the capital of Mongolia?
9) What South American country has Pacific and Atlantic coastlines?
10) What is the most northern African country?

Quiz 1 Answers

1) Ecuador
2) Aconcagua – 22,841 feet in Argentina
3) Dogs – The name comes from the Latin "canaria" for dog; when the first Europeans arrived, they found large dogs on Gran Canaria.
4) China – 13,743 miles and 14 countries
5) United States
6) Chile
7) Huron – 23,012 square miles
8) Ulaanbaatar
9) Colombia
10) Tunisia

Quiz 2

1) What is the lowest average elevation continent?
2) By area, what is the largest of the Canadian provinces and territories?

3) What country has the world's longest road tunnel?

4) What city has the world's busiest McDonald's restaurant?

5) By area, what is the world's fifth largest country?

6) What is the highest active volcano in the world?

7) By area, what is the largest lake in South America?

8) What is the largest island in the Arctic Ocean?

9) What country has the most volcanoes (active and extinct)?

10) What is the smallest ocean?

Quiz 2 Answers

1) Australia – 984 feet average elevation

2) Nunavut – 808,200 square miles

3) Norway – 15.2 miles

4) Moscow, Russia

5) Brazil

6) Ojos Del Salado – 22,595 feet on the Chile and Argentina border

7) Maracaibo – 5,100 square miles

8) Baffin - 195,928 square miles

9) United States – 173

10) Arctic

Quiz 3

1) What Central American country extends furthest north?

2) What capital city is on the slopes of the volcano Pichincha?

3) How many locks are there on the Suez Canal?

4) What country has the highest average elevation?

5) What two Canadian provinces are landlocked?

6) What two countries have square flags?

7) What is the only river that crosses the equator in both a northerly and southerly direction?

8) What European country has the longest coastline?

9) At over 9,000 miles in length, what country's Highway 1 forms a complete loop along its borders?

10) What is the second largest island in Europe?

Quiz 3 Answers

1) Belize
2) Quito, Ecuador
3) Zero
4) Bhutan – 10,760 feet average elevation
5) Alberta and Saskatchewan
6) Switzerland and Vatican City
7) Congo
8) Norway
9) Australia
10) Iceland – 39,702 square miles

Quiz 4

1) What is the least densely populated country in the world?
2) From what South American country does the Orinoco River flow into the Atlantic Ocean?
3) What country does China have its longest land border with?
4) By area, what is the smallest continent?
5) The Canary Islands are part of what country?
6) What is the second largest city in England?
7) What river is known as China's Sorrow?
8) What is the longest canal in the world?
9) What European country has no single head of state?
10) By area, what is the largest island in Asia?

Quiz 4 Answers

1) Mongolia – Areas like Greenland have even lower density, but they aren't independent countries.
2) Venezuela
3) Mongolia
4) Australia
5) Spain

6) Birmingham

7) Yellow – due to its devastating floods

8) Grand Canal of China – 1,104 miles

9) Switzerland

10) Borneo – 287,000 square miles

Quiz 5

1) What country has the third largest English speaking population?

2) By area, what is the largest Mediterranean island?

3) What country has the fourth largest population?

4) By volume, what is the largest lake in South America?

5) What country took its name from a line of latitude?

6) What country's phone book is alphabetized by first name?

7) What is the most populous country the equator passes through?

8) What is the highest elevation capital city in Europe?

9) What country issued the first Christmas stamp in 1898?

10) What is the world's most northerly national capital city?

Quiz 5 Answers

1) Pakistan

2) Sicily – 9,927 square miles

3) Indonesia

4) Lake Titicaca

5) Ecuador

6) Iceland – Everyone is referenced by their first name; they don't have surnames in the traditional sense; the surname is their father's first name suffixed with either son or daughter.

7) Indonesia

8) Madrid – 2,188 feet

9) Canada

10) Reykjavik, Iceland – 64 degrees north latitude

Quiz 6

1) What was the last province to become part of Canada?

2) What is the longest river in Asia?

3) What is the world's largest gulf?

4) How many oceans are there and what are their names?

5) What is the world's most southerly national capital?

6) What is the second longest river in North America?

7) What country has the longest coastline?

8) What is the world's highest elevation national capital city?

9) What peninsula does Mexico occupy?

10) Alphabetically, what country comes between Portugal and Romania?

Quiz 6 Answers

1) Newfoundland

2) Yangtze – 3,915 miles

3) Gulf of Mexico – 600,000 square miles

4) Five – Atlantic, Pacific, Indian, Arctic, Southern

5) Wellington, New Zealand – 41 degrees south latitude

6) Mississippi – 2,320 miles

7) Canada

8) La Paz, Bolivia – 11,942 feet

9) Yucatan

10) Qatar

Quiz 7

1) By area, what is the second largest island in Asia?

2) By area, what is the largest landlocked country?

3) How many countries are there in South America?

4) By area, what is the fourth largest continent?

5) Zanzibar lies off the coast of what country?

6) What is the driest continent?

7) What is the world's widest river?

8) In what location are most of the world's geysers found?

9) What island has the highest maximum elevation?

10) What is the highest mountain in Canada?

Quiz 7 Answers

1) Sumatra, Indonesia – 164,000 square miles
2) Kazakhstan - ninth largest country
3) 12
4) South America
5) Tanzania
6) Antarctica – about eight inches of precipitation annually
7) Amazon – from 7-25 miles wide depending on season
8) Yellowstone National Park, Wyoming
9) New Guinea – 16,024 feet
10) Mt. Logan – 19,551 feet in the Yukon territory

Quiz 8

1) By area, what is the largest body of fresh water in the world?
2) What percent of the Earth's fresh water is in the Antarctic ice sheet?
3) What is the shallowest ocean?
4) What is the driest non-polar desert in the world?
5) What mountain range spans northern Morocco, Algeria, and Tunisia?
6) By area, what is the largest archipelago (chain or group of islands scattered across a body of water)?
7) By area, what is the second largest country in the world?
8) What is the most populous city south of the equator?
9) What is the capital of Qatar?
10) By area, what is the smallest North American country?

Quiz 8 Answers

1) Lake Superior – 31,700 square miles
2) 90% - It is equivalent to about 230 feet of water in the world's oceans.
3) Arctic – average depth of 3,407 feet

4) Atacama – Chile
5) Atlas Mountains
6) Malay Archipelago – 25,000 islands making up Indonesia and the Philippines
7) Canada
8) Sao Paulo, Brazil
9) Doha
10) St. Kitts and Nevis – 101 square miles in the Caribbean

Quiz 9

1) How many landlocked countries are there in the world?
2) What is the second most populous city in Asia?
3) In which country is the Great Victoria Desert?
4) By area, what is the smallest Canadian province?
5) What sea is located between Australia and New Zealand?
6) By area, what is the largest country in Africa?
7) What country would you have to visit to see the ruins of Troy?
8) By area, what is the largest lake that is entirely within Canada?
9) What European country has the lowest population density?
10) What is the deepest lake in North America?

Quiz 9 Answers

1) 44 - Afghanistan, Andorra, Armenia, Austria, Azerbaijan, Burundi, Burkina Faso, Bhutan, Belarus, Bolivia, Botswana, The Central African Republic, Chad, The Czech Republic, Ethiopia, Hungary, Kazakhstan, Kyrgyzstan, Laos, Lesotho, Liechtenstein, Luxembourg, Malawi, Moldova, Mongolia, Macedonia, Mali, Nepal, Niger, Paraguay, Rwanda, Serbia, San Marino, Switzerland, Slovakia, Swaziland, South Sudan, Tajikistan, Turkmenistan, Uganda, Uzbekistan, Vatican City, Zambia, Zimbabwe
2) Jakarta, Indonesia
3) Australia
4) Prince Edward Island
5) Tasman
6) Algeria

7) Turkey

8) Great Bear Lake – 12,028 square miles

9) Iceland

10) Great Slave Lake in Canada – 2,015 feet deep

Quiz 10

1) What country has the largest number of islands?

2) By area, what is the smallest Central American country?

3) What two South American countries are landlocked?

4) By area, what is the world's largest fresh water island?

5) What is the second longest river in Africa?

6) What country has the most forest land?

7) What country has the most countries or territories bordering it?

8) What is Europe's second longest river?

9) What national capital city has views of the volcano Snaefellsjokull?

10) What country has the world's highest railroad?

Quiz 10 Answers

1) Finland – over 100,000

2) El Salvador

3) Bolivia and Paraguay

4) Manitoulin – over 1,000 square miles in Lake Huron in Ontario, Canada

5) Congo – 2,922 miles

6) Russia

7) China – 14 countries and 2 territories

8) Danube – 1,777 miles

9) Reykjavik, Iceland

10) China – 16,640 feet

Quiz 11

1) By area, what is the largest country entirely in Europe?

2) How many countries border the Black Sea?

3) By area, what is the largest country with English as an official language?

4) There are only two predominantly Christian countries in Asia; the smaller is East Timor; what is the other?

5) What is the most populous city in India?

6) The source of the Amazon river is in what country?

7) What is the coldest national capital city in the world?

8) Timbuktu is in what country?

9) What river rises in Tibet and flows through China, Myanmar, Laos, Thailand, Cambodia, and Vietnam?

10) What European country has the highest population density?

Quiz 11 Answers

1) Ukraine - 223,000 square miles

2) Six - Turkey, Georgia, Russia, Ukraine, Romania, Bulgaria

3) Canada

4) Philippines – fourth largest Christian population in the world and third largest Roman Catholic

5) Mumbai

6) Peru

7) Ulaanbaatar, Mongolia – Winter temperatures of minus 40 degrees Fahrenheit are not unusual.

8) Mali – west Africa

9) Mekong

10) Monaco – over 47,000 per square mile

Quiz 12

1) What desert covers most of southern Mongolia?

2) By volume, what is the largest freshwater lake?

3) What sacred volcano last erupted in 1707?

4) What is the world's warmest sea?

5) In the boot shaped country of Italy, what region comprises the toe?

6) What is the world's oldest surviving sovereign state?

7) What country has three capital cities?

8) What name is given to a ring shaped coral reef?

9) What is the only Central American country that has English as its official language?

10) What is the name of the deepest known ocean location?

Quiz 12 Answers

1) Gobi

2) Lake Baikal in Russia – It has a maximum depth of 5,387 feet and contains about 20% of the total unfrozen surface freshwater in the world.

3) Mount Fuji

4) Red Sea

5) Calabria

6) San Marino - 301 AD

7) South Africa - Pretoria is the administrative capital; Cape Town is the legislative capital, and Bloemfontein is the judicial capital.

8) Atoll

9) Belize

10) Challenger Deep in the Mariana Trench in the Pacific Ocean – 36,070 feet deep

Quiz 13

1) How many provinces does Canada have?

2) What is the saltiest ocean?

3) What is the only sea without a coastline (no land border)?

4) Mount Kosciuszko is the highest mountain on what continent?

5) What country has the lowest average elevation?

6) What is the longest river in Australia?

7) Which of the Great Lakes doesn't share a border with Canada?

8) What country and its territories cover the most time zones?

9) What percent of the world's population lives in the Northern Hemisphere?

10) What country has the oldest surviving constitution?

Quiz 13 Answers

1) 10 - Alberta, British Columbia, Manitoba, New Brunswick, Newfoundland and Labrador, Nova Scotia, Ontario, Prince Edward Island, Quebec, Saskatchewan

2) Atlantic

3) Sargasso Sea – It is in the North Atlantic Ocean off the coast of the U.S. and is defined by currents.

4) Australia

5) Maldives – 1,200 mostly uninhabited islands in the Indian Ocean; average elevation is 6 feet.

6) Murray River – 1,558 miles

7) Lake Michigan

8) France with 12 time zones – The U.S. and Russia each cover 11 time zones.

9) 88% - About half of the world's population lives north of 27 degrees north latitude.

10) San Marino – 1600

Quiz 14

1) By area, what is the largest country that the equator passes through?

2) What country has the most pyramids?

3) Where is the lowest dry land point in the world?

4) What is the only continent without an active volcano?

5) What country is Transylvania in?

6) The country of San Marino is completely surrounded by what country?

7) What country has the most official languages?

8) What country has the most lakes?

9) How many countries does the equator pass through?

10) What is the only country that falls in all four hemispheres?

Quiz 14 Answers

1) Brazil

2) Sudan – almost twice as many as Egypt

3) Dead Sea – 1,411 feet below sea level

4) Australia

5) Romania

6) Italy

7) Zimbabwe – 16

8) Canada – It has more lakes than the rest of the world combined.

9) 13 - Ecuador, Colombia, Brazil, Sao Tome & Principe, Gabon, Republic of the Congo, Democratic Republic of the Congo, Uganda, Kenya, Somalia, Maldives, Indonesia, Kiribati

10) Kiribati - island nation in the Central Pacific Ocean

Quiz 15

1) What is widely regarded as the oldest continuously inhabited city in the world?

2) By discharge volume, what is the largest river in the world?

3) Europe is separated from Asia by what mountain range?

4) Excluding Greenland, what is the easternmost point of the North American continent?

5) What country has the world's deepest cave?

6) How many time zones does Russia have?

7) What is the largest desert in the world?

8) South Africa completely surrounds what other country?

9) What strait separates Europe and Asia?

10) What is the largest country that uses only one time zone?

Quiz 15 Answers

1) Damascus, Syria – at least 11,000 years

2) Amazon

3) Ural Mountains

4) Cape Spear, Newfoundland, Canada

5) Georgia – Krubera Cave, explored to a depth of 7,208 feet

6) 11

7) Antarctic Polar Desert – 5.5 million square miles

8) Lesotho

9) Bosporus

10) China – Geographically, it has five time zones, but it chooses to use one standard time.

Quiz 16

1) What two countries share the longest land border?

2) What Canadian province or territory is closest to the North Pole?

3) What is the only European national capital not on a river?

4) Valletta is the capital of what country?

5) What color is most common on national flags?

6) What country has the most active volcanoes?

7) By volume, what is the world's largest active volcano?

8) What is the capital of Australia?

9) What is Europe's largest island?

10) What non-landlocked country has the shortest coastline?

Quiz 16 Answers

1) United States and Canada – 5,525 miles

2) Nunavut

3) Madrid, Spain

4) Malta

5) Red

6) Indonesia – 76 active volcanoes

7) Mauna Loa, Hawaii

8) Canberra

9) Great Britain

10) Monaco – 2.4 miles

Quiz 17

1) What country has the largest Christian population?

2) What country has the largest Muslim population?

3) What is the second longest river in South America?

4) By area, what is the second largest country in South America?

5) By area, what is the largest lake in Africa?

6) What country has the second largest English speaking population?

7) In what country is the highest point that the equator passes through?

8) What country has the largest Spanish speaking population?

9) What is the second largest landlocked country?

10) What country has the lowest birthrate?

Quiz 17 Answers

1) United States

2) Indonesia

3) Parana – 3,032 miles

4) Argentina – 1,073,518 square miles

5) Victoria – 26,564 square miles

6) India

7) Ecuador – 15,387 feet

8) Mexico

9) Mongolia

10) Monaco

Quiz 18

1) The U.S. and China have the first and second largest GDP's; what country is third?

2) How many countries have effectively 100% literacy rates?

3) What country has the most international tourists annually?

4) Based on land area, what is the largest airport in the world?

5) What is the most visited city in the world?

6) What is the largest cocoa producing country?

7) Brazil is the largest coffee producing country; what country is second?

8) By area, how many of the 10 largest countries in the world are in Asia?

9) How many of the 10 most populous countries in the world are in

Asia?

10) What is the driest place in the world?

Quiz 18 Answers

1) Japan
2) Five – Andorra, Finland, Liechtenstein, Luxembourg, Norway
3) France
4) King Fahd International, Saudi Arabia - 301 square miles
5) Bangkok, Thailand – followed by London
6) Ivory Coast (Cote d'Ivoire)
7) Vietnam
8) Four – Russia, China, India, Kazakhstan
9) Seven – China, India, Indonesia, Pakistan, Bangladesh, Russia, Japan
10) McMurdo Dry Valleys, Antarctica – row of snow free valleys that haven't seen water in millions of years

Quiz 19

1) What are the only three countries that have Atlantic and Mediterranean coasts?
2) How many countries are completely surrounded by one other country?
3) What is the only continent with land in all four hemispheres?
4) What continent has the most freshwater?
5) What ocean has about 75% of the world's volcanoes?
6) What country has the largest city in the world based on land area?
7) What is the only major city located on two continents?
8) What country has the world's longest freshwater beach?
9) What is the most populous city in Europe?
10) What is the most populous city in Asia?

Quiz 19 Answers

1) France, Spain, Morocco
2) Three – Lesotho (surrounded by South Africa), Vatican City and San

Marino (both surrounded by Italy)
3) Africa
4) Antarctica – The ice sheet contains about 90% of world's fresh water.
5) Pacific
6) China – The city of Hulunbuir is 102,000 square miles.
7) Istanbul, Turkey
8) Canada – Wasaga Beach on the shores of Lake Huron is 14 miles long.
9) Moscow, Russia
10) Tokyo, Japan

Quiz 20

1) What is the most populous city in North America?
2) What two countries have the second longest shared land border?
3) What city has the most millionaires in the world?
4) What country consumes the most electricity in the world?
5) What city has the most skyscrapers in the world?
6) What is the sunniest city in the world?
7) What two countries produce a majority of the world's vanilla?
8) Astana is the capital of what country?
9) What is the most frequently crossed international border in the world?
10) What country is in the eastern Pyrenees between France and Spain?

Quiz 20 Answers

1) Mexico City
2) Russia and Kazakhstan – 4,254 miles
3) Tokyo, Japan
4) China - followed by U.S. and Russia
5) Hong Kong - followed by New York City and Dubai
6) Yuma, Arizona – On average, the sun shines 90% of daylight hours.
7) Madagascar and Indonesia
8) Kazakhstan

9) United States and Mexico

10) Andorra

Quiz 21

1) What country has the world's longest fence?
2) What three South American countries does the equator pass through?
3) The Anatolian peninsula makes up most of what country?
4) What place on the Earth is closest to the Moon?
5) Of the 25 highest mountain peaks in the world, how many are in the Himalayas?
6) What is the only country in the world without an official capital?
7) What country has the world's tallest vertical cliff?
8) What continent has the most countries?
9) What country has the third most countries bordering it?
10) What is the most populous Canadian province?

Quiz 21 Answers

1) Australia – The dingo fence completed in 1885 is 3,488 miles long.
2) Ecuador, Colombia, Brazil
3) Turkey
4) Mount Chimborazo, Ecuador – It is 20,548 feet elevation but very close to the equator, so the bulge in the Earth makes it 1.5 miles closer than Mount Everest.
5) 19
6) Nauru – third smallest country in the world in the Central Pacific Ocean with less than 10,000 people
7) Canada – Mount Thor on Baffin Island with a 4,101 feet vertical drop
8) Africa – 54, Europe – 47, Asia – 44
9) Brazil – 10
10) Ontario

Quiz 22

1) Outside of Warsaw, what city has the largest Polish population in

the world?

2) Taumatawhakatangihangakoauauotamateaturipukakapikimaunga-horonukupokaiwhenuakitanatahu has what distinction?

3) How many people have been to the deepest part of the ocean?

4) The word Canada comes from an Indian word meaning what?

5) What is the only continent without a major desert?

6) What is the longest river in Canada?

7) What is different about how the flag of the Philippines is flown?

8) Amman, the capital of Jordan, was previously named what?

9) Russia is the most populous country in Europe; what country is second?

10) What country is the largest wine producer in the world?

Quiz 22 Answers

1) New York City

2) Longest place name in the world – a hill in New Zealand

3) Three – Director James Cameron is one of them.

4) Village or settlement

5) Europe

6) Yukon – 1,981 miles

7) It is displayed with the blue side up in times of peace and with the red side up in times of war.

8) Philadelphia – after Philadelphus, the Egyptian king who conquered the area in the third century BC

9) Germany

10) Italy - followed by Spain, France, U.S.

Quiz 23

1) What is the second largest island in North America?

2) The Eiffel Tower was originally intended for what city?

3) What European national capital city is built on 14 islands?

4) At the closest point, Europe and Africa are separated by what distance?

5) Almost half the gold ever mined has come from what single

location?

6) What continent has the most French speakers?

7) What is the only country to lie completely above 1,000 meters elevation?

8) What is the windiest continent?

9) What city has the largest taxi fleet in the world?

10) What country has the highest annual average hours worked in the world?

Quiz 23 Answers

1) Baffin – 195,928 square miles

2) Barcelona – Spain rejected the project.

3) Stockholm, Sweden

4) Nine miles – across the Strait of Gibraltar between Spain and Morocco

5) Witwatersrand, South Africa

6) Africa – 120 million French speakers

7) Lesotho

8) Antarctica

9) Mexico City

10) Mexico

Quiz 24

1) What is the most linguistically diverse (highest number of languages spoken) city in the world?

2) Technically, who is the largest land owner in the world?

3) By area, how many of the 10 largest countries in the world are in South America?

4) The United Kingdom and Great Britain are not the same; what is the difference?

5) Brazil borders all but what two South American countries?

6) What city was the only European capital outside of Europe?

7) What is the most populous democratic country?

8) What country has the largest number of languages spoken?

9) What is the only country in the world named after a woman?

10) What is the smallest population country with at least one Nobel Prize winner?

Quiz 24 Answers

1) New York City – 800 languages

2) Queen Elizabeth II – She technically owns 6.6 billion acres or about 1/6 of the world's land including Canada and Australia.

3) Two – Brazil and Argentina

4) Great Britain includes England, Scotland, and Wales; the United Kingdom includes those countries plus Northern Ireland.

5) Chile and Ecuador

6) Rio de Janeiro, Brazil was capital of Portugal from 1808 to 1822 – Napoleon was invading Portugal at the time, so the Portuguese royal family moved to Rio de Janeiro, and it became the capital.

7) India

8) Papua New Guinea – about 840 languages or one for every 10,000 citizens

9) St. Lucia – It is named after St. Lucy of Syracuse.

10) Faroe Islands – with 50,000 people located halfway between Norway and Iceland

Quiz 25

1) What national capital city has the smallest percent of the country's population?

2) What continent has the largest volcanic region on Earth?

3) How many debt free countries are there in the world?

4) How many countries in the world require their head of state to be a specific religion?

5) What is the only Asian country the equator passes through?

6) Is the Northern or Southern Hemisphere warmer?

7) How many countries don't maintain an army?

8) What location has the most lightning strikes in the world?

9) By population, what is the world's largest island country?

10) What country has on average the tallest people?

Quiz 25 Answers

1) Washington, D.C., United States – 0.21% of the U.S. population
2) Antarctica – an area of over 100 volcanoes under the ice sheet in western Antarctica
3) Five - Macau, British Virgin Islands, Brunei, Liechtenstein, Palau
4) 30
5) Indonesia
6) Northern – 2.7 degrees Fahrenheit warmer due to ocean circulation
7) 22 – including Andorra, Costa Rica, Panama, Grenada, Haiti, Iceland, Liechtenstein
8) Lake Maracaibo, Venezuela - Lightning storms occur for about 10 hours a night, 140 to 160 nights a year, for a total of about 1.2 million lightning discharges per year.
9) Indonesia
10) Netherlands – average 6 feet ½ inches for men and 5 feet 7 inches for women

Quiz 26

1) What country has on average the shortest people?
2) How many landlocked countries are there in North America?
3) What is the largest city in the Caribbean?
4) What is the largest city in Central America?
5) What is the southernmost city in the world with a population over 1 million?
6) What is the northernmost city in the world with a population over 1 million?
7) By area, what is the smallest country in South America?
8) By area, what is the smallest country in Africa?
9) By area, what is the largest lake in Europe?
10) By area, what is the smallest country in Asia?

Quiz 26 Answers

1) Indonesia – average 5 feet 2 inches for men and 4 feet 10 inches for women

2) Zero

3) Santo Domingo, Dominican Republic

4) Guatemala City, Guatemala

5) Melbourne, Australia – 37.8 degrees south latitude

6) St. Petersburg, Russia – 59.9 degrees north latitude

7) Suriname – 63,252 square miles

8) Seychelles – Group of 115 islands covering 177 square miles and lying 932 miles east of mainland Africa

9) Ladoga – 6,834 square miles in Russia

10) Maldives – 115 square mile group of 26 islands in the Indian Ocean

Quiz 27

1) What is the most populous country in Central America?

2) How many countries are in North America?

3) What is the only continent without glaciers?

4) What is the largest island in the world formed solely by volcanic activity?

5) How many landlocked countries are there in Europe?

6) What is the longest freshwater lake in the world?

7) What continent has the most landlocked countries?

8) What is the longest river in North America?

9) What is the highest mountain outside Asia?

10) By area, what is the world's smallest mountain range?

Quiz 27 Answers

1) Guatemala

2) 23 – Antigua and Barbuda, Bahamas, Barbados, Belize, Canada, Costa Rica, Cuba, Dominica, Dominican Republic, El Salvador, Grenada, Guatemala, Haiti, Honduras, Jamaica, Mexico, Nicaragua, Panama, St. Kitts and Nevis, St. Lucia, St. Vincent and the Grenadines, Trinidad and Tobago, United States

3) Australia

4) Iceland – 39,768 square miles

5) 14 - Andorra, Austria, Belarus, Czech Republic, Hungary, Liechtenstein, Luxembourg, Macedonia, Moldova, San Marino,

Serbia, Slovakia, Switzerland, Vatican City
6) Tanganyika – 420 miles in Africa
7) Africa – 16
8) Missouri – 2,341 miles
9) Aconcagua – 22,841 feet in Argentina
10) Sutter Buttes in the northern Great Valley of central California - 75 square miles with maximum elevation of 2,122 feet

Quiz 28

1) By area, what is the largest country in the Southern Hemisphere?
2) By volume, what is the second largest freshwater lake in the world?
3) What country is the fourth largest in the Americas (North and South America)?
4) What is the largest island in North America?
5) What two countries share Victoria Falls in Africa?
6) What African country was divided in two in 2011?
7) What country has the highest asphalt road in the world?
8) What is the highest navigable lake in the world?
9) What city of at least 1 million population is furthest away from another city of at least 1 million population?
10) What is the most remote (furthest from the nearest land) island in the world?

Quiz 28 Answers

1) Brazil – A small portion is in the Northern Hemisphere.
2) Tanganyika – maximum depth of 4,820 feet
3) Argentina
4) Greenland – 836,300 square miles
5) Zambia and Zimbabwe
6) Sudan – now Sudan and South Sudan
7) China (Tibet) – 18,258 feet
8) Lake Titicaca – 12,507 feet elevation in Bolivia and Peru
9) Auckland, New Zealand – 1,347 miles away from Sydney, Australia
10) Bouvet Island in the South Atlantic Ocean - 994 miles to Antarctica

Quiz 29

1) By discharge volume, what is the second largest river in the world?
2) The point in the oceans furthest from the nearest land is called what?
3) Germany is closest in size to what U.S. state?
4) Greenland is a territory of what country?
5) By area, what is the largest island nation?
6) What Canadian province borders the most states?
7) What European country is divided into areas called cantons?
8) By area, what is the largest country with Spanish as an official language?
9) What is the largest lake in Antarctica?
10) What country has the second largest Spanish speaking population?

Quiz 29 Answers

1) Congo
2) Point Nemo – It is in the South Pacific Ocean 1,670 miles from the nearest land.
3) Montana – Germany is 137,983 square miles; Montana is 147,040 square miles.
4) Denmark
5) Indonesia – 735,358 square miles
6) Ontario – borders five states - Minnesota, Michigan, Ohio, Pennsylvania, New York
7) Switzerland
8) Argentina
9) Lake Vostok – largest of the subglacial lakes
10) United States

Quiz 30

1) What is the highest waterfall in the world?
2) The world's largest pyramid by volume is in what country?
3) What is the most common symbol on flags of the world?
4) What country is last alphabetically?

5) What country is first alphabetically?

6) Why is the city of La Paz, Bolivia one of the most fire safe cities?

7) What river flows through eight countries and four national capitals?

8) What is the deepest lake in the world?

9) What are Africa's four great rivers?

10) The Somers Islands have what more familiar name?

Quiz 30 Answers

1) Angel Falls, Venezuela – 3,212 feet high

2) Mexico – The Great Pyramid of Cholula has a base of 450 meters each side and a height of 66 meters.

3) Star

4) Zimbabwe

5) Afghanistan

6) At an elevation of 11,800 feet, it is difficult for fires to spread due to the low oxygen level.

7) Danube

8) Lake Baikal, Russia – 5,387 feet deep

9) Nile, Congo, Zambezi, Niger

10) Bermuda

Quiz 31

1) What national capital city is heated by volcanic springs?

2) By area, what is the world's largest island?

3) By area, Vatican City is the world's smallest country; what is the second smallest?

4) What is the world's longest mountain range?

5) What country has the world's second largest Christian population?

6) What is the most populous African country?

7) What is the only country crossed both by the equator and Tropic of Capricorn?

8) What is the largest desert in the Western Hemisphere?

9) By area, what is the largest island in South America?

10) By area, what is the largest Canadian province?

Quiz 31 Answers

1) Reykjavik, Iceland
2) Greenland – 836,300 square miles
3) Monaco – 0.78 square miles
4) Andes – 4,300 miles
5) Brazil
6) Nigeria
7) Brazil
8) Patagonian Desert – 258,688 square miles primarily in Argentina
9) Tierra del Fuego – 18,605 square miles
10) Quebec – 595,400 square miles

Quiz 32

1) What is the second longest river in Asia?
2) What country has the highest per capita electricity consumption?
3) What is the oldest national capital city in the Americas?
4) What is the northernmost Scandinavian country?
5) What major city is on an island in the St. Lawrence River?
6) By area, what is the world's largest sea?
7) What is the only Middle Eastern country without a desert?
8) **What is the largest enclosed inland body of water in the world?**
9) What river goes over Victoria Falls?
10) What is the most populous city in Africa?

Quiz 32 Answers

1) Yellow – 3,395 miles
2) Iceland – more than four times higher than the U.S.
3) Mexico City – founded in 1521
4) Norway
5) Montreal, Canada
6) Philippine – 2.2 million square miles

7) Lebanon
8) Caspian Sea – It is considered a lake by some, but it has salt water and has 3.5 times more water than all the Great Lakes combined covering 143,244 square miles.
9) Zambezi
10) Lagos, Nigeria

Quiz 33

1) What country has the southernmost point in continental Europe?
2) What national capital city does the River Liffey flow through?
3) By area, what is the second largest continent?
4) What is the only Dutch speaking country in South America?
5) What is Abyssinia now called?
6) What national capital rises where the Blue Nile and White Nile converge?
7) Of all meteorites ever found, 90% come from what continent?
8) What two cities are at the ends of the Trans-Siberian railroad?
9) What four seas are named for colors?
10) By area, what is the second largest island in the world?

Quiz 33 Answers

1) Spain
2) Dublin, Ireland
3) Africa
4) Suriname – former Dutch colony
5) Ethiopia
6) Khartoum, Sudan
7) Antarctica
8) Moscow and Vladivostok
9) Red, Black, Yellow, White
10) New Guinea – 303,476 square miles

Quiz 34

1) By volume, what is the world's largest volcano (active or extinct)?

2) What continent has the highest population density?

3) What is Europe's longest river?

4) What continent has the highest average elevation?

5) By area, what is the smallest of the Great Lakes?

6) What country has the world's highest elevation city?

7) What peninsula do Spain and Portugal share?

8) What is the longest river in the Americas?

9) By area, what is the largest country in Central America?

10) What country's flag has lasted the longest without change?

Quiz 34 Answers

1) **Tamu Massif** – extinct volcano 1,000 miles east of Japan under the Pacific Ocean

2) Asia

3) Volga – 2,294 miles

4) Antarctica – 8,200 feet average elevation

5) Lake Ontario – 7,320 square miles

6) Peru – La Rinconada is a mining town at 16,700 feet in the Andes and has about 30,000 residents.

7) Iberian

8) Amazon – 4,345 miles

9) Nicaragua – 50,338 square miles

10) Denmark – 1370 or earlier

Quiz 35

1) What country has the largest Portuguese speaking population?

2) What country's flag is incorporated most often in other flags?

3) What African capital city is named for a U.S. president?

4) **What is the northernmost country in continental South America?**

5) What country has the most tornadoes?

6) By area, what is the largest Scandinavian country?

7) What country has the most earthquakes?

8) How many Canadian provinces border the Great Lakes?

9) What country has the world's southernmost city?

10) What is the official language of Nigeria?

Quiz 35 Answers

1) Brazil
2) Great Britain
3) Monrovia, Liberia
4) **Colombia**
5) United States
6) Sweden
7) Indonesia – followed by Japan
8) One – Ontario
9) Chile
10) English

Quiz 36

1) Which of the Great Lakes do all the others flow into?
2) What continent has the lowest highest point?
3) How many landlocked countries are there in Asia?
4) What is the world's most populous metropolitan area?
5) What is the second most widely spoken language in the world?
6) The land location furthest from any ocean is in what country?
7) How many Australian states are there?
8) What is the capital of Monaco?
9) Switzerland has four official languages; what are they?
10) What river flows through Rome?

Quiz 36 Answers

1) Lake Ontario
2) Australia - Mount Kosciuszko at 7,310 feet
3) 12 - Afghanistan, Armenia, Azerbaijan, Bhutan, Laos, Kazakhstan, Kyrgyzstan, Mongolia, Nepal, Tajikistan, Turkmenistan, Uzbekistan
4) Tokyo, Japan

5) Spanish – Mandarin is first; English is third.

6) China – 1,645 miles from the ocean near the Kazakhstan border in extreme northwestern China

7) Six – New South Wales, Queensland, South Australia, Tasmania, Victoria, Western Australia

8) Monaco – It is both a city and a country.

9) German, French, Italian, and Romanish, a romance language spoken predominantly in one canton

10) Tiber

Quiz 37

1) What two South American countries share the region of Patagonia?

2) What is the smallest population country with two or more Nobel Prize winners?

3) What is Australia's island state?

4) What country contains South America's highest and lowest points?

5) What is the world's highest mountain that isn't part of a range?

6) By area, what is the smallest country in the Australian continent?

7) By area, what is the largest country entirely within the Southern Hemisphere?

8) What two countries contain Sierra Nevada mountains?

9) By area, what is the largest Japanese island?

10) What was Canada's first national park?

Quiz 37 Answers

1) Chile and Argentina

2) St. Lucia – Caribbean island with 185,000 people and two Nobel Prize winners

3) Tasmania

4) Argentina – 22,841 feet above sea level to 344 feet below

5) Mount Kilimanjaro, Tanzania – 19,341 feet

6) Nauru – eight square miles

7) Australia – A small portion of Brazil is in the Northern Hemisphere.

8) United States and Spain

9) Honshu – 87,182 square miles

10) Banff National Park

Quiz 38

1) What is the most populous city north of the Arctic Circle?

2) What is the most populous country with English as an official language?

3) Mount Chogori is better known by what name?

4) In what country is the only point on the equator with snow on the ground?

5) If you flew due east from New York City, what is first foreign country you would reach?

6) What two bodies of water does the Suez Canal connect?

7) What is the most populous city in Canada?

8) What language is the official language of the most countries?

9) What country spans the Pacific Ocean, Caribbean Sea, Amazon River, and Andes Mountains?

10) What is the largest island on the Australian continent?

Quiz 38 Answers

1) Murmansk, Russia – over 300,000 people at 69 degrees north latitude

2) India

3) K2 – second highest mountain in the world

4) Ecuador

5) Portugal

6) Red Sea and Mediterranean Sea

7) Toronto

8) English – 54 countries

9) Colombia

10) New Guinea – 303,476 square miles

Quiz 39

1) Besides Antarctica, what continent has the lowest population density?

2) What is Canada's oldest city?

3) What is the largest island in the Indian Ocean?

4) What are the only two countries completely surrounded by landlocked countries?

5) What is the only country that borders both the Caspian Sea and the Persian Gulf?

6) What is Canada's second most populous city?

7) What is the most populous country in the Southern Hemisphere?

8) What is the only country with a two-sided (different designs on each side) flag?

9) What is the second most populous Canadian province?

10) What is the third most populous country in Europe?

Quiz 39 Answers

1) Australia

2) Quebec - 1608

3) Madagascar – 226,658 square miles

4) Uzbekistan and Liechtenstein

5) Iran

6) Montreal

7) Indonesia

8) Paraguay

9) Quebec

10) Turkey

CPSIA information can be obtained
at www.ICGtesting.com
Printed in the USA
BVHW032052050420
576912BV00001B/43